DEDICATION

This glossary is dedicated to our patients. May this explanation of terms foster better understanding of mental disorders and of persons afflicted by them.

a psychiatric glossary
THE MEANING OF TERMS
FREQUENTLY USED IN PSYCHIATRY

Edited by the Subcommittee of the Committee on
Public Information

Shervert H. Frazier, M.D., *Chairman*
Robert J. Campbell, M.D.
Myron H. Marshall, M.D.
Arnold Werner, M.D.

Robert L. Robinson, M.A., *Staff Consultant*
Jane E. Edgerton, M.A., *Staff Consultant*

Fourth Edition
American Psychiatric Association
1975
Basic Books, Inc., Publishers   New York

TABLE OF CONTENTS

PRESENTING THE FOURTH EDITION

The American Psychiatric Association takes pride in presenting this *Fourth Edition* of *A Psychiatric Glossary* which has proven so useful to approximately 800,000 persons in the mental health field since the first edition appeared in 1957.

It is of interest that the *First Edition* contained somewhat fewer than 500 definitions, nearly all of them derived from "dynamic psychiatry". The *Second Edition* in 1964 added about 150 new terms chiefly from the maturing fields of psychopharmacology, neurophysiology, biochemistry, and community psychiatry.

Now, in the *Fourth Edition*, approximately 400 new terms have been added. A great many of them have been grouped together into Tables—*legal terms, schools of psychiatry, research, psychological tests, sleep disorders, neurologic deficits, drugs used in psychiatry*—a device which we think will enhance its effectiveness as a book of reference. Also, a truly comprehensive list of definitions in *behavior therapy* is now included.

Thus, the successive editions of the *Glossary* reflect directions of growth and progress in psychiatry. May the *Fifth Edition*, about five years hence, reflect comparable progress!

The Association is grateful to the Subcommittee that prepared this *Fourth Edition* comprising Drs. Shervert H. Frazier (Chairman), Robert J. Campbell, Myron H. Marshall, and Arnold Werner, with Mr. Robert L. Robinson and Ms. Jane Edgerton as Staff Consultants and similarly to the members of the Committee on Public Information since 1956 who were responsible for the earlier editions. We are also indebted to many colleagues in other disciplines who generously volunteered their expert advice and suggestions.

John P. Spiegel, M.D.
President
American Psychiatric Association

ACKNOWLEDGMENTS

The *Fourth Edition* would not have been possible without the assistance of many experts in psychiatry and related fields. We are grateful to them all.

Very special thanks are due Stephanie B. Stolz, Ph.D. for the definition of terms used in *behavior therapy*, to Alan A. Stone, M.D. for the *Table of Legal Terms,* and to Bryan T. Woods, M.D. for the *Table of Neurologic Deficits.* The *Table on Sleep Disorders* is based on material from "Clinical Disorders of Sleep" by R. L. Williams and I. Karacan in *Sleep and Clinical Practice* (Gene Usdin, Editor, Brunner Mazel, N.Y., 1973), and "Sleep Disorders" by A. Kales and J. D. Kales, *New England Journal of Medicine,* 290:487-499, 1974.

Other scholars who contributed various definitions or to the editing thereof include: Ross J. Baldessarini, M.D., Alan L. Bateman, M.P.H., M.D., Arnold S. Berkman, Ph.D., Dietrich Blumer, M.D., Barbara J. Brandt, M.A., Leonard Cammer, M.D., John A. Capell, Ph.D., Jonathan O. Cole, M.D., Joseph Coppala, M.D., Stanley Dean, M.D., Norbert B. Enzer, M.D., Horacio Fabrega, Jr., M.D., Charlotte F. Fritzke, R.N., M.S.W. Warren J. Gadpaille, M.D., Donald W. Hammersley, M.D., Leo E. Hollister, M.D., Dan Kesselbrenner, Alexander Leighton, M.D., Ira S. Lerwin, M.D., Harold Lief, M.D., Petter Lindstrom, M.D., Barbara Marshall, Ed.D., N. L. Mintz, Ph.D., Silvio Onesti, M.D., Bruce E. Pailler, M.A., J. Christopher Perry, M.P.H., M.D., Saul H. Rosenthal, M.D., Ralph Ryback, M.D., Claire F. Seigel, Ed.D., Joseph Schildkraut, M.D., Mogens Schou, M.D., Ira Sherwin, M.D., Herbert Spiegel, M.D., Thomas W. Stach, M.D., Ian Stevenson, M.D., Mary C. Sweeney, Bernard S. Yudowitz, M.D., LLB., Jack Zusman, M.D., M.P.H.

We also wish to thank Ms. Elouise B. Rhone of the APA Staff for her superb diligence and expertness in typing the manuscript for the printer.

7

TO THE READER

The words that appear in *italics* in this glossary are also defined in it, making it convenient for the reader to crosscheck one reference with another. At times the italicized word is listed alphabetically in a closely related form. For example, "psychotic" is not listed but *psychosis* is. In the tables, words that appear in **bold face type** are defined elsewhere in the table or in the alphabetical listing in the glossary.

A

ability: Capability; competence; power to do or perform an act. Ability implies the capacity to perform the act without further training, while the term *aptitude* implies that the potential capacity is present but requires training to bring it to a specific level of ability.

abreaction: Emotional release or discharge resulting from recalling to awareness a painful experience that has been forgotten (repressed) because it was consciously intolerable. A therapeutic effect sometimes occurs through partial discharge of the painful emotions, desensitization to them, and increased insight.

abstinence: Voluntarily denying oneself some kind of gratification; in the area of *drug dependence*, the state of being without the drug on which the subject is dependent. The "abstinence syndrome" is equivalent to *withdrawal symptoms*, and its appearance suggests the presence of physiological dependence or *addiction*.

abstinence, sexual: Voluntary nonengagement in sexual intercourse; continence.

abstract attitude (categorical attitude): Includes such abilities as the following: assuming a mental set voluntarily; shifting voluntarily from one aspect of a situation to another; keeping in mind simultaneously various aspects of a situation; grasping the essentials of a whole, breaking a whole into its parts, and isolating them voluntarily; planning ahead ideationally; assuming an attitude to the merely possible; thinking or performing symbolically. A characteristic of many psychiatric patients is the inability to

9

assume the abstract attitude, or to shift readily from the concrete to the abstract and back again as demanded by the circumstances.

abulia: See *Table of Neurologic Deficits*, p. 72.

abused child syndrome: See *battered child syndrome*.

acalculia: See *Table of Neurologic Deficits*, p. 72.

accident prone: Special susceptibility to accidents which are based on psychological causes or motivations.

accreditation: In medicine, a process by which hospitals are surveyed and approved by the *Joint Commission on Accreditation of Hospitals* as measured against standards set by the Commission. Private and public mental hospitals and community mental health centers are accredited by an Accreditation Council for Psychiatric Facilities which operates under the aegis of the JCAH.

acrophobia: See *phobia*.

acting out: Expressions of *unconscious* emotional conflicts or feelings of hostility or love in actions rather than words. The individual is not *consciously* aware of the meaning of such acts. May be harmful or, in controlled situations, therapeutic (e.g. children's play therapy).

acute confusional state: See *organic brain syndrome*.

acute situational or stress reactions: See *gross stress reaction*.

adaptation: Fitting or conforming to the environment, typically by means of a combination of autoplastic maneuvers (which involve a change in the self) and alloplastic maneuvers (which involve alteration of the external environment). The end result of successful adaptation is termed *adjustment*. "Maladjustment" refers to unsuccessful attempts at adaptation.

addiction: Dependence on a chemical substance to the extent that physiologic dependence is established. The latter manifests itself as *withdrawal symptoms* (the *abstinence* syndrome) when the drug is withdrawn. Narcotics, alcohol, and most sedative drugs may produce addiction. See also *drug dependence*.

adiadochokinesia: See *Table of Neurologic Deficits*, p. 72.

10

adjustment: The relation between the person, his inner self, and his environment. See also *adaptation*.

Adler, Alfred (1870-1937): Viennese *psychiatrist*. See *individual psychology, inferiority complex* (under *complex*), *compensation*, and *overcompensation*.

adolescence: A chronological period beginning with the physical and emotional processes leading to sexual and psychosocial maturity and ending at an ill-defined time when the individual achieves independence and social productivity. The period is associated with rapid physical, psychological and social changes. For purposes of discussion, adolescence is often divided into early, mid, and late periods. See also *psychosocial development* and *psychosexual development*.

adrenergic: Referring to neural activation by *catecholamines* such as *epinephrine, norepinephrine*, and *dopamine*. See also *sympathetic nervous system* and *biogenic amines*.

aerophagia: Excessive air swallowing.

affect: A person's emotional feeling tone and its outward manifestations. Affect and *emotion* are commonly used interchangeably.

affective disorder: Any *mental disorder* in which a disturbance of *affect* is predominant. This broad concept includes *depressive neurosis*, the *major affective disorders*, and *psychotic depressive reaction*. See *depression* and *manic depressive psychosis*.

aftercare: See *community psychiatry*.

aggression: A forceful physical, verbal, or symbolic action. May be appropriate and self-protective, including healthful self-assertiveness, or inappropriate. Also may be directed outward toward the environment, as in *explosive personality*, or inward toward the self, as in *depression*.

agitated depression: A psychotic *depression* accompanied by constant restlessness. Sometimes seen in *involutional melancholia*. See also *depression*.

agitation: Severe restlessness; a major psychomotor expression of emotional tension.

11

agnosia: See *Table of Neurologic Deficits*, p. 72.

agoraphobia: See *phobia*.

agraphia: See *Table of Neurologic Deficits*, p. 72.

ailurophobia: See *phobia*.

akathisia: See *Table of Neurologic Deficits*, p. 72.

akinetic mutism: See *Table of Neurologic Deficits*, p. 72.

Alanon: An organization of relatives of alcoholic individuals operated in many communities under the philosophical and organizational structure of *Alcoholics Anonymous* to facilitate discussion and resolution of common problems.

Alcohol, Drug Abuse, and Mental Health Administration (ADAMHA): A government agency within the U.S. Department of Health, Education, and Welfare responsible for administering federal grant programs to advance and support research, training, and service programs in the areas of *alcoholism, drug abuse,* and *mental health.*

> **National Institute on Alcohol Abuse and Alcoholism:** An institute within ADAMHA, responsible for programs dealing with alcohol abuse and *alcoholism.*

> **National Institute on Drug Abuse:** An institute within ADAMHA, responsible for programs dealing with *narcotic* and *drug abuse.*

> **National Institute of Mental Health:** An institute within ADAMHA, responsible for programs dealing with *mental health.*

alcoholic hallucinosis: A *psychosis* characterized by threatening auditory *hallucinations* occurring without disorientation during periods of alcohol intake. This disorder is thought to represent the disinhibition by alcohol of underlying *psychopathology.* Contrast with *delirium tremens.*

alcoholic psychoses: A group of major mental disorders associated with organic brain damage and caused by poisoning from alcohol. Includes *delirium tremens, Wernicke-Korsakoff syndrome,* and often *alcoholic hallucinosis.* See also *Table of Sleep Disorders,* p. 84.

12

Alcoholics Anonymous (AA): The name of a group composed of former alcoholics who collectively assist alcoholics through personal and group support. See also *Al-Teen* and *Alanon*.

alcoholism: A chronic disease manifested by repeated drinking that produces injury to the drinker's health or to his social or economic functioning.

alexia: See *Table of Neurologic Deficits*, p. 72. See also *dyslexia*.

algophobia: See *phobia*.

alienation: The term is used to denote the state of estrangement the individual feels in cultural settings that he views as foreign, unpredictable, or unacceptable. For example, in *depersonalization* phenomena, feelings of unreality or strangeness produce a sense of alienation from one's self or environment. In *obsessions*, where there is fear of one's emotions, avoidance of situations that arouse emotions, and continuing effort to keep feelings out of awareness, there is alienation of *affect*.

alienist: Obsolete term of historical significance for a *psychiatrist* who testifies in court about a person's sanity or mental competence.

allied health professional: An individual with special training, working under the supervision of a health professional with responsibilities bearing on patient care.

alpha feedback, alpha state: See *biofeedback*.

Al-Teen: An organization of teenaged children of alcoholic parents operated in some communities under the philosophical and organizational structure of *Alcoholics Anonymous*. It provides a setting in which the children may receive group support in achieving a better understanding of their parents' problems and better methods for coping with them.

Alzheimer's disease: A pre-senile degenerative *organic brain disease* probably due to multiple *etiologies*. The symptoms are similar to *Pick's disease*.

ambivalence: The coexistence of two opposing *drives*, desires, feelings, or *emotions* toward the same person, object, or goal. These may be *conscious* or partly conscious; or one side of the feelings

13

may be *unconscious.* Example: love and hate toward the same person.

ambulatory schizophrenia: A term for a person with schizophrenia who functions sufficiently well that he generally does not require hospitalization. If in a hospital, he is kept on open wards or he may be allowed the complete freedom of the community.

American Journal of Psychiatry: The official monthly scientific journal of the *American Psychiatric Association.*

American Law Institute Formulation: See *Table of Legal Terms,* p. 70.

American Psychiatric Association: The leading national professional organization in the United States for physicians who specialize in *psychiatry.* It also includes members from Canada, Central America, and the Caribbean Islands, and corresponding members from other countries. Founded in 1844 as the Association of Medical Superintendents of American Institutions for the Insane, the Association changed its name to the American Medico-Psychological Association in 1891, and adopted its present name in 1921. The Association is governed by a board of 19 elected trustees whose primary function is to formulate and implement the policies and programs of the Association, and by an Assembly of District Branches representing the membership which may approve or disapprove, but not reverse, actions of the Board of Trustees. Numerous councils, committees, and task forces furnish the data and recommendations on which the Trustees and Assembly base their deliberations. The Association had 22,000 members in 1974. Its headquarters are at 1700 18th Street, N.W., Washington, D.C. 20009.

amimia: Inability to gesticulate or to understand the significance of gestures. See *speech disturbances, learning disabilities.*

amines: Organic compounds containing the amino group ($-NH_3$). Of special importance in biochemistry and neurochemistry. See also *biogenic amines* and *catecholamines.*

amnesia: Pathological loss of memory; forgetting; a phenomenon in which an area of experience is forgotten and becomes inaccessible to *conscious* recall. It may be of organic, emotional, or mixed origin, and limited to a sharply circumscribed period of time.

14

anterograde amnesia: Amnesia for events that occurred after a significant point in time.

retrograde amnesia: Amnesia for events that occurred before a significant point in time.

amok: See *culture specific syndromes.*

amphetamines: A group of chemicals that stimulate the cerebral cortex of the brain. Often misused by adults and adolescents to control normal fatigue and to induce *euphoria.* Used clinically to treat *hyperkinetic syndrome, narcolepsy,* and as an adjunctive treatment in *depressions.*

anaclitic: Literally, leaning on. In psychoanalytic terminology, denotes dependence of the infant on the mother or mother substitute for his sense of well being (e.g. gratification through nursing). Normal in childhood; pathologic in later years if excessive.

anaclitic depression: An acute and striking impairment of an infant's physical, social, and intellectual development that sometimes occurs following a sudden separation from the mothering person. See also *depression.*

anal character: A personality type that manifests excessive orderliness, miserliness, and obstinacy. In *psychoanalysis*, a pattern of behavior in an adult that is believed to originate in the *anal phase* of infancy. See *psychosexual development.*

anal phase: See *psychosexual development.*

analgesia: Absence of appreciation of painful sensations.

analysand: A patient in psychoanalytic treatment.

analysis: A common synonym for *psychoanalysis.*

analytic psychology: The name given by the Swiss psychoanalyst, Carl Gustav *Jung* (1875-1961), to his theoretical system, which minimizes the influence of sexual factors in emotional disorders and stresses mystical religious influences. See also *Jung.*

anamnesis: The developmental history of an individual and of his illness, especially a patient's recollections.

15

anankastic personality: A synonym for *obsessive compulsive personality*. See *personality disorders*.

anesthesia: Absence of sensation; may result from nerve damage, anesthetic drugs, or psychological processes such as in *hysterical neurosis, conversion type* (see under *neurosis*) or *hypnosis*.

anhedonia: Chronic inability to experience pleasure. See also *hedonistic*.

anima: In Jungian psychology, the inner being of an individual as opposed to the outer character or *persona* that he presents to the world. Further, the anima may be the more feminine "soul" or inner self of a man; the animus the more masculine soul of a woman. See also *Jung*.

anomie: Apathy, alienation, and personal distress resulting from the loss of goals previously valued. Durkheim popularized this term when he listed it as one of the principal reasons for suicide.

anorexia nervosa: A syndrome marked by severe and prolonged inability to eat, with marked weight loss, amenorrhea (or impotence), and other symptoms resulting from emotional conflict and biological changes. Most frequently encountered in girls and young women. Also see *Table of Sleep Disorders*, p. 84.

anosognosia: See *Table of Neurologic Deficits*, p. 72.

Antabuse (disulfiram): A drug used in treatment of *alcoholism*. It blocks the normal metabolism of alcohol and produces increased blood concentrations of acetaldehydes which cause very unpleasant reactions including pounding of the heart, shortness of breath, nausea, and vomiting.

antianxiety drugs: See *Table of Drugs Used in Psychiatry*, p. 68.

antidepressants: See *Table of Drugs Used in Psychiatry*, p. 68.

antimanic drugs: See *Table of Drugs Used in Psychiatry*, p. 68.

antipsychotic drugs: See *Table of Drugs Used in Psychiatry*, p. 68.

antisocial personality: See *personality disorders*.

anxiety: Apprehension, tension, or uneasiness that stems from the anticipation of danger, the source of which is largely unknown or unrecognized. Primarily of intrapsychic origin, in distinction to fear, which is the emotional response to a *consciously* recognized and usually external threat or danger. Anxiety and fear are accompanied by similar physiologic changes. May be regarded as pathologic when present to such extent as to interfere with effectiveness in living, achievement of desired goals or satisfactions, or reasonable emotional comfort. See also *panic*.

anxiety hysteria: An early psychoanalytic term for what is now called *phobic neurosis*. See under *neurosis*.

anxiety neurosis: See under *neurosis*.

aphasia: See *Table of Neurologic Deficits*, p. 72.

aphonia: Inability to produce normal speech sounds. May be due to either organic or psychic causes.

apoplexy: See *stroke*.

apperception: Perception as modified and enhanced by the individual's own *emotions*, memories, and biases.

apraxia: See *Table of Neurologic Deficits*, p. 72.

aptitude: See *ability*.

assertive training: See under *behavior therapy*.

association: Relationship between ideas or *emotions* by contiguity, continuity, or by similarity. See also *free association* and *mental status*.

astereognosis: See *Table of Neurologic Deficits*, p. 72.

asthenic personality: See *personality disorders*.

attributable risk: See *Table of Research Terms*, p. 74.

aura: A premonitory, subjective sensation (e.g. a flash of light) that often warns the person of an impending headache or convulsion. Seen in *migraine* and *epilepsy*.

autism (autistic thinking): A form of thinking marked by extreme self-absorption and egocentricity, in which objective facts are

17

obscured, distorted or excluded in varying degrees. This symptom can appear in adults or children. See also *early infantile autism*.

autoeroticism: Sensual self-gratification. Characteristic of, but not limited to, an early stage of emotional development. Includes satisfactions derived from genital play, *masturbation*, fantasy, and from oral, anal, and visual sources.

automatism: Automatic and apparently undirected behavior that is not *consciously* controlled. Seen in *psychomotor epilepsy*. See under *epilepsy*.

autonomic nervous system: The part of the nervous system that innervates the cardiovascular, digestive, reproductive, and respiratory organs. It operates outside of consciousness and controls basic life-sustaining functions such as the heart rate, digestion, and breathing. It includes the *sympathetic nervous system* and the *parasympathetic nervous system*.

autotopagnosia: See *Table of Neurologic Deficits*, p. 72.

aversion therapy: See *aversive control* under *behavior therapy*.

aversive control: See under *behavior therapy*.

aversive stimulus: See *reinforcement* under *behavior therapy*.

B

barbiturates: See *Table of Drugs Used in Psychiatry*, p. 68.

battered child syndrome (abused child syndrome): A child or infant who has suffered repeated injuries, often including fractures and neurologic damage, at the hands of a parent, or parents, or parent *surrogates.* The beatings take place over a period of time and are often precipitated by minor and normal irritating behavior of the child. The abusive parent has a low threshold for frustration and poor impulse control. Such parents often have had marked deprivation in their own childhood and were abused themselves.

Bayley Scales of Infant Development: See *Table of Psychological Tests*, p. 78.

Beers, Clifford W. (1876-1943): Author of *A Mind That Found Itself* and founder, in 1909, of the National Committee for Mental Hygiene, now the *National Association for Mental Health.*

behavior disorders of childhood: A group of behavior patterns occurring in childhood and *adolescence* that are less severe than *psychoses* but more resistant to treatment than *transient situational disturbances* because they are more stabilized and internalized. They are characterized by overactivity, inattentiveness, shyness, feelings of rejection, over-aggressiveness, timidity, or delinquency. The child who runs away from home or who persistently lies, steals, and teases other children in a hostile fashion falls into this category.

behavior modification: See *behavior therapy.*

behavior therapy: (behavior modification, conditioning therapy): Any treatment approach designed to modify the patient's behavior directly, rather than correct the dynamic causation. Behavior therapy is derived from laboratory investigations of learning and focuses on modifying observable and, at least in principle, quantifiable behavior by means of systematic manipulation of the environmental and behavioral variables thought to be functionally related to the behavior. Some of the many techniques included within behavior therapy are: *operant conditioning, shaping, token economy, systematic desensitization, aversive control, assertive training, flooding, implosion.* See also *biofeedback.*

assertive training: A form of *behavior therapy* in which patients are taught appropriate interpersonal responses, involving frank, honest, and direct expression of their feelings, both positive and negative.

19

aversive control: The use of stimuli that are unpleasant to the patient, as a means of changing his inappropriate behavior. These *behavior therapy* techniques are used only with the consent of the patient or his guardians. Aversive control methods include *aversion therapy* and *punishment techniques.* These methods have been most successful when used in combination with other procedures that strengthen desirable behavior.

aversion therapy: A *behavior therapy* treatment based on *respondent conditioning.* Stimuli associated with undesirable behavior are paired with a painful or unpleasant stimulus, resulting in the suppression of the undesirable behavior. For example, the look, smell, and taste of alcoholic beverages would be paired with nausea induced by emetics, so that the patient felt conditioned nausea when around alcoholic beverages, thus suppressing his drinking of them. See also therapy by *reciprocal inhibition.*

conditioning (learning): A more or less permanent change in an individual's behavior that occurs as a result of experience and practice. Conditioning is employed clinically in *behavior therapy.* There are generally considered to be two types of conditioning, *operant conditioning* and *respondent conditioning.*

operant conditioning (instrumental conditioning): A process according to which the environmental events (*reinforcers*) following the individual's behavior determine whether the behavior is more or less likely to occur in the future. Through *shaping,* the individual learns to make new responses. Through *differential reinforcement,* the individual learns to make some responses more frequently, others less. The process of *extinction* results in the behavior returning to its pre-conditioning level. These principles and related procedures are used in *behavior therapy* to teach patients new, appropriate behavior, and to eliminate undesirable behavior. See also *reinforcement, stimulus control.*

respondent conditioning (classical conditioning, Pavlovian conditioning): A process as a result of which a response mediated primarily by the *autonomic nervous system* (an "unconditioned response," such as salivation or a change in

20

heart rate) comes to occur in the presence of a stimulus that normally does not elicit that response (a neutral stimulus, such as the sound of a bell). In respondent conditioning, the neutral stimulus is repeatedly presented just before the presentation of a stimulus that normally elicits that response in an untrained individual (an *unconditioned stimulus*). When the autonomic response occurs regularly in the presence of the neutral stimulus alone, the response is called a "conditioned response," and the formerly neutral stimulus, a *conditioned stimulus*. When the conditioned stimulus is frequently presented alone, without the unconditioned stimulus, the conditioned response ceases to be elicited by it. This process is known as "respondent extinction." See also *stimulus control*.

desensitization: See *systematic desensitization*.

discriminative stimulus: An environmental event correlated with *reinforcement*. This stimulus comes to exercise a controlling function over the behavior, so that the behavior tends to occur mainly in the presence of the environmental event. For example, if only a particular staff person gives out the tokens when patients in a *token economy* socialize, the patients will tend to socialize only when that person is around. The staff member is a discriminative stimulus for the desirable behavior.

extinction: When a learned operant response is no longer followed by a *reinforcer*, it will eventually return to the level of strength characterizing it before it was altered by the positive or negative reinforcer. This process is termed extinction; behavior that has been subjected to extinction is said to be extinguished.

differential reinforcement: A procedure in which desirable behavior is followed by positive *reinforcement*. In contrast, undesirable or less desirable behavior is extinguished or punished.

flooding: A *behavior therapy* for *phobias* and other problems involving maladaptive *anxiety*, in which *aversive stimuli* are presented in intense forms, either in imagination or in real life. Usually the emotional responses cease to occur after several trials. See also *implosion*.

21

generalization: The process resulting in behavior occurring in an environment in which it has not previously been *reinforced*.

implosion: A *behavior therapy* for *phobias*, in which the patient is presented repeatedly with vivid accounts of hazardous consequences that can be produced by the object he fears. The presentations are continued until the object is no longer fearful and the *anxiety* does not occur.

punishment techniques: *Behavior therapy* techniques based on *operant conditioning*. One method, punishment, involves the addition of an *aversive stimulus* after the inappropriate behavior. For example, a strong aversive stimulus applied immediately after self-injurious behavior has been shown to eliminate it. Another punishment technique involves the removal of a positive stimulus after the inappropriate behavior. For example, a patient engaging in an undesirable act might temporarily lose a privilege. With either of these *aversive control* techniques, so long as the patient does not perform the undesirable behavior, he is able to avoid being punished.

reciprocal inhibition: The conceptual basis for some forms of *behavior therapy*. According to this theory, if responses that inhibit *anxiety* can be made to occur in the presence of anxiety-provoking stimuli, the bond between those stimuli and the anxiety will be weakened. For example, assertive responses are used in *assertive training* to overcome anxieties associated with social interaction, and relaxation responses are used in *systematic desensitization* to decrease the anxiety associated with various stimuli.

reinforcement: The strengthening of a response. This process is central in *operant conditioning*. When a stimulus, added to the environment, strengthens the immediately preceding response, the response is said to have undergone positive reinforcement. When a stimulus, subtracted from the environment, strengthens the immediately preceding response, the response is said to have undergone negative reinforcement. If the stimulus is one that at some time in the individual's life could not strengthen responses and has acquired reinforcing power, the process is called conditioned reinforcement.

22

reinforcer (reinforcing stimulus): A stimulus that, when presented, acts to strengthen a response. If the stimulus, when added to the environment, strengthens the immediately preceding response, it is called a positive reinforcer. If the stimulus, when subtracted from the environment, strengthens the immediately preceding response, it is called a negative reinforcer or *aversive stimulus.* A stimulus that has acquired reinforcing power it formerly did not have, is called a *conditioned reinforcer.* An example of a positive conditioned reinforcer is money; an example of a negative conditioned reinforcer is social censure.

schedule of reinforcement: A rule that specifies which occurrences of a particular operant response will be followed by a *reinforcer.* A reinforcer does not have to follow every occurrence of an operant response in order for it to be maintained, and, in fact, intermittency in the occurrence of reinforcers is the most common state of affairs.

shaping: A procedure used in *behavior therapy* to teach new behavior. Responses in the patient's repertoire that are most like the desired behavior are *reinforced.* The behavior that is reinforced is then gradually changed to approximate the desired pattern more closely. Responses less close to the desired one undergo *extinction.* For example, in treating a patient who has severe anxieties in interpersonal situations, the therapist might begin by reinforcing simple social skills similar to those already in the patient's repertoire, such as making eye contact and smiling, and then go on, in small steps, to teach increasingly complex social behavior, such as greeting others and extending invitations.

stimulus control: In *conditioning,* a general term used to describe the influence that environmental events have over behavior. Some examples of stimulus control are:

conditioned stimulus: A formerly neutral environmental event that now elicits an *autonomic* response, as a result of the association of the neutral event with an *unconditioned stimulus.* For example, a bell does not naturally elicit salivation; if the bell is frequently paired with food in the mouth, the bell alone will come to elicit salivation. See also *respondent conditioning*.

discrimination: The process resulting in behavior occurring in only some stimulus settings. *Autonomic* responses will be elicited by *conditioned stimuli* that have been paired with *unconditioned stimuli,* and not by stimuli that are different from the conditioned stimuli. Operant behavior will occur in environments in which it has been reinforced, but not in environments very different from those associated with reinforcement. For example, if a response is reinforced in the patient's home but not elsewhere, it will be strong at home and unlikely to occur elsewhere.

eliciting stimulus: An environmental event that elicits an *autonomic* response. *Unconditioned stimuli* and *conditioned stimuli* are eliciting stimuli.

unconditioned stimulus: An environmental event that naturally elicits an *autonomic* response. For example, food in the mouth elicits salivation.

systematic desensitization (desensitization): A widely used form of *behavior therapy,* involving training in deep muscle relaxation, the construction of *anxiety* hierarchies, and the counterposing of relaxation with the anxiety-evoking stimuli from the hierarchies. This method has generally proved successful in modifying emotional behavior associated with *phobias, frigidity, insomnia,* and other problems.

token economy: A work-payment incentive system involving the application of the principles and procedures of *operant conditioning* to the management of a social setting such as a ward, classroom or halfway house. Conditioned *reinforcers,* such as tokens, points, or credits, are given to the patients when they engage in desired behavior; these tokens are then exchanged for any of an array of positive reinforcers, such as store items, activities, and privileges. The goal of the program is to develop appropriate behavior. The tokens bridge the gap between the appropriate behavior and the reinforcement.

behavioral science(s): Those sciences focused on the study of man's development, interpersonal relationships, values, experiences, activities, and institutions, such as *psychiatry, psychology,* cultural anthropology, sociology, political science, and *ethology.*

behaviorism: An approach to *psychology* first developed by John B. *Watson.* In its original form, behaviorism rejected the notion of mental states and insisted on reducing all psychological phenomena to neural, muscular, and glandular responses. Contemporary behaviorism also emphasizes the study of observable responses, but is directed toward general behavior rather than discrete acts. Contemporary behaviorism includes private events such as feelings and *fantasies,* to the extent that these can be indirectly observed and measured.

Bender Visual-Motor Gestalt Test: See *Table of Psychological Tests,* p. 78.

Benton Visual Retention Test: See *Table of Psychological Tests,* p. 78.

bestiality: Sexual relations between human and animal. See *sexual deviation.*

biofeedback: Provision of information to the subject based on one or more of his physiologic processes, such as brainwave activity or blood pressure, often as an essential element in visceral learning, or learning to control physiologic processes even though they produce no *consciously* perceived sensations (also known as physiologic self-regulation).

The work of experimental psychologist Neal E. Miller and his associates, however, has shown that visceral reactions, reflexes and similar processes that are under *autonomic nervous system* control are also subject to learning *(learned autonomic control),* even though not *conscious* and not under the control of the somatic nervous system.

Instrumental or *operant conditioning,* refers to the fact that immediate rewards influence subsequent behavior, that patterns of behavior which are instrumental in satisfying needs and relieving pain or stress tend to be repeated. Because vital functions, such as blood pressure, are never maintained at an absolutely constant level, their fluctuations can be treated as responses and reinforced

25

appropriately (rewarded), so that the subject can learn to control his internal organ function even though he may not consciously understand how such learning has been achieved (*operant autonomic conditioning*).

Alpha brain waves (7.5-13.5 cps) characterize relaxed and peaceful wakefulness, which is accordingly known as the alpha state. Alpha biofeedback training attempts to teach the subject to achieve a state of relaxation by giving him information on his *EEG*. In one technique, an acoustic tone sounds in the absence of alpha waves; when the subject produces alpha waves, the tone disappears.

Similar results in relaxation training and control of states of consciousness are achieved with transcendental meditation. In this technique the subject repeats a mantra (a Sanskrit syllable or word) over and over until he is so relaxed that even the mantra disappears from consciousness. If the subject starts to have disturbing thoughts, he begins again to repeat the mantra until he is relaxed. He usually continues in that state for 15 to 20 minutes.

Such techniques have excited interest because of their possible application to large groups of psychiatric patients as antianxiety agents that are under control of patients, and as ways of affecting physiologic processes that have psychologic and emotional analogues (*psychosomatic* disorders, for example).

biogenic amines: Organic substances of interest because of their possible role in brain functioning. Subdivided into *catecholamines* (e.g. *epinephrine, dopamine, norepinephrine*) and the *indoleamines* (e.g. *tryptophan, serotonin*).

biogenic amine hypothesis: The concept, derived mainly from neurobiology and *psychopharmacology* that *amines* including the *catecholamines* and *serotonin*, acting as synaptic neurotransmitters in the *CNS*, and subserving important aspects of emotion, states of consciousness, responses to stress and related behaviors, may be abnormal in certain psychiatric illnesses. In particular, the increased activity of *norepinephrine* has been suggested to occur in *mania*, and the converse in endogenous depression. Overactivity of *dopamine* has been postulated in *schizophrenia* and childhood *hyperkinesis*. Activity of *antidepressant drugs* and *antipsychotic drugs* seems best explained by their ability to potentiate or block the actions of biogenic amines in the brain, respectively.

biological psychiatry: A school of psychiatric thought that emphasizes physical, chemical, and neurological causes and treatment approaches. It includes social, psychodynamic, and other knowledge of human behavior. See *Table of Schools of Psychiatry*, p. 77.

biological rhythms: Cyclical variations in physiologic and biochemical function, level of activity and emotional state. Circadian rhythms have a cycle of about 24 hours. Ultradian rhythms are shorter than one day and infradian rhythms are longer than one day and may be weeks or months.

bipolar psychosis: An *affective disorder* in which there are both manic and depressive episodes in the same person. Also called *manic-depressive psychosis, circular type.*

birth trauma: Term used by Otto *Rank* to relate his theories of *anxiety* and *neurosis* to the inevitable psychic shock of being born.

bisexuality: Originally a concept of *Freud's* indicating the belief that components of both sexes could be found in each individual. Today the term is often used to refer to persons who are capable of achieving *orgasm* with a partner of either sex. See also *gender role, homosexuality.*

Bleuler, Eugen (1857-1939): Swiss *psychiatrist* whose investigations of *dementia praecox* led him to outline the modern concept of *schizophrenia.*

blocking: A sudden obstruction or interruption in the train of thought or speech perceived by the person as an absence or deprivation of thought. Although normal persons may occasionally experience blocking, it is commonly seen in a variety of mental disorders and most often in *schizophrenia.*

board certified psychiatrist: A *psychiatrist* who has taken and passed examinations administered by the American Board of Psychiatry and Neurology, and thus become certified as a medical specialist in psychiatry.

board eligible psychiatrist: A *psychiatrist* who is eligible to take the examinations of the American Board of Psychiatry and Neurology; basically, a psychiatrist who has completed an approved three-year residency training program and two additional years of approved experience in the field.

body language: The message (s) transmitted by a person's body motion, which is a learned form of communication that has meaning within the context in which it appears. Linguistics, the study of words and language, and *kinesics*, the study of body posture, movement and facial expression, are directed toward the isolation and analysis of infracommunication systems as a way to reduce the data of interactional behavior to objective, significant, measurable and manipulatable units. See *kinesics, kinesiology*.

borderline state (borderline psychosis): An unofficial diagnostic term for a condition in which a person's symptoms are difficult to classify as either *psychotic* or nonpsychotic. The symptoms may shift quickly from one pattern to another, and often include *acting out* and behavior suggesting *schizophrenia*. See *latent schizophrenia* under *schizophrenia*.

bradykinetic syndrome: Neurological state characterized by a generalized slowness of all motor activity and a lack or disturbance of spontaneous movements characteristic of normal individuals.

brain disorders: See *organic brain syndrome*.

brain syndrome: See *organic brain syndrome*.

brain waves: See *electroencephalogram*.

Brawner decision: See American Law Institute Formulation in *Table of Legal Terms*, p. 70.

brief psychotherapy: Any form of *psychotherapy* the end point of which is defined either in terms of the number of sessions (generally, not more than 20), or in terms of specified objectives. Brief therapy is usually goal-oriented, circumscribed, active, focused, and may be directive.

Brigham, Amariah (1798-1849): One of the original thirteen founders of the *American Psychiatric Association* (1844) and the founder and first editor of its official journal, now the *American Journal of Psychiatry*.

bruxism (teeth grinding). See *Table of Sleep Disorders*, p. 84.

bulimia: Morbidly increased hunger. Same as *polyphagia*. Seen at times in *anorexia nervosa*.

butyrophenones: See *Table of Drugs Used in Psychiatry*, p. 68.

C

carbon dioxide treatment: See *shock treatment*.

care and protection proceedings: See *Table of Legal Terms*, p. 70.

caregiver: Any person involved in the identification or prevention of illness or in the treatment or rehabilitation of the patient. Included are the primary physician or front-line caregiver (the person to whom the patient comes initially for help), the consultant or specialist, and the indigenous worker (the person from the patient's own group or culture who has had special training or experience in one or more areas of health care). Community caregivers provide a pseudofamily for many patients who have no supporting family of their own. Sometimes called community workers, mental health workers, and *allied health professionals*.

castration: Removal of the sex organs. In psychological terms, the fantasied loss of the penis. Also used figuratively to denote state of *impotence*, powerlessness, helplessness, or defeat.

castration anxiety: *Anxiety* due to fantasied danger or injuries to the genitals and/or body. May be precipitated by everyday

29

events which have symbolic significance and appear to be threatening such as loss of job, loss of a tooth, or an experience of ridicule or humiliation.

castration complex: A group of emotionally charged ideas that are *unconscious* and which refer to the fear of losing the genital organs, usually as punishment for forbidden sexual desires; includes the childhood fantasy that female genitals result from loss of a penis.

catalepsy: A generalized condition of diminished responsiveness usually characterized by trance-like states. May occur in organic or psychological disorders, or under *hypnosis.*

cataplexy: See *Table of Sleep Disorders*, p. 84.

catatonic state (catatonia): A state characterized by immobility with muscular rigidity or inflexibility and at times by excitability. See *schizophrenia.*

catchment area: Used in psychiatry to delineate a geographic area for which a mental health facility has responsibility. See *community psychiatry.*

catecholamines: A group of *biogenic amines* derived from phenylalanine and containing the catechol nucleus. Certain of these amines, such as *epinephrine, norepinephrine,* and *dopamine,* exert an important influence on nervous system activity.

categorical attitude: See *abstract attitude.*

catharsis: The healthful (therapeutic) release of ideas through a "talking out" of *conscious* material accompanied by the appropriate emotional reaction. Also, the release into awareness of repressed (i.e. "forgotten") material from the *unconscious.*

cathexis: Attachment, *conscious* or *unconscious,* of emotional feeling and significance to an idea or object, most commonly a person.

Cattell Infant Intelligence Scale: See *Table of Psychological Tests*, p. 78.

causalgia: A sensation of burning pain of either organic or psychic origin.

central nervous system (CNS): The brain and spinal cord.

central (syntactical) aphasia: See *Table of Neurologic Deficits,* p. 72.

cephalalgia: Headache or head pain.

cerea flexibilitas: The "waxy flexibility" often present in catatonic *schizophrenia* in which the patient's arm or leg remains passively in the position in which it is placed.

cerebral arteriosclerosis: Hardening of the arteries of the brain sometimes resulting in an *organic brain syndrome* that may be either primarily neurologic in nature (e.g. convulsions, *aphasia*, chorea, athetosis, *parkinsonism*, etc.), or primarily mental (e.g. intellectual dulling, memory deficits, emotional *lability, paranoid delusions,* confusion, and finally profound *dementia*), or a combination of both. Cerebral arteriosclerosis typically manifests itself in persons over 50 years of age.

cerebral electrotherapy (CET): A low intensity electrical treatment usually employing positive pulses of direct current. Used primarily in the treatment of *insomnia, anxiety,* and neurotic *depression. Electrosleep* is a synonym.

cerebral vascular accident: See *stroke.*

CET: *Cerebral electrotherapy.*

character: The sum of the relatively fixed *personality* traits and habitual modes of response of an individual.

character analysis: Psychoanalytic treatment aimed at the *character defenses.*

character defense: Any character or *personality* trait which serves an *unconscious* defensive purpose. See also *defense mechanism.*

character disorder: A *personality disorder* manifested by a chronic and habitual pattern of reaction that is maladaptive in that it is relatively inflexible, limits the optimal use of potentialities, and often provokes the very counterreactions from the environment that the subject seeks to avoid. In contrast to symptoms of *neurosis,* character traits are typically *egosyntonic.* See also *personality.*

character neurosis: Similar to *character disorder* except that the *neurotic conflicts* are expressed in exaggerated but socially acceptable patterns of behavior and may not be easily recognizable as symptoms.

child abuse: See *battered child syndrome.*

child analysis: Application of modified *psychoanalytic* methods and goals to problems of children to remove impediments to normal personality development.

Child's Apperception Test (CAT): See *Table of Psychological Tests,* p. 78.

childhood schizophrenia: See *schizophrenia.*

chlorpromazine: See *Table of Drugs Used in Psychiatry,* p. 68.

cholinergic: Activated or transmitted by acetylcholine (e.g. parasympathetic nerve fibers). See also *parasympathetic nervous system.* Contrast with *adrenergic.*

chromosomes: Microscopic intranuclear structures that carry the *genes.* The normal human cell contains 46 chromosomes.

circadian rhythms: See *biological rhythms.*

clang associations: A type of thinking in which the sound of a word, rather than its meaning, gives the direction to subsequent associations; punning and rhyming may substitute for logic, and language may become more and more a senseless *compulsion* to associate and less and less a vehicle for communication. Clang associations have been most frequently reported in *manic* states and in *schizophrenic* disorders.

classical conditioning: See *conditioning* under *behavior therapy.*

claustrophobia: See *phobia.*

climacteric: Menopausal period in women. Also used sometimes to refer to the corresponding age period in men.

clinical psychologist: See *psychologist, clinical.*

CMHC: See *community mental health center.*

CNS: See *central nervous system.*

cognitive: Referring to the mental process of comprehension, judgment, memory, and reasoning, as contrasted with emotional and volitional processes. Contrast with *conative.*

cognitive development: The progress of the individual beginning in infancy, in the acquisition of intelligence, *conscious* thought and problem solving abilities. An orderly sequence in the increase in knowledge derived from sensorimotor activity has been empirically demonstrated by Jean *Piaget.* See also: *psychosexual development* and *psychosocial development.*

collective unconscious: In Jungian theory, a portion of the *unconscious* common to all humans; also called "racial unconscious." See *unconscious* and *Jung.*

coma: See *organic brain syndrome.*

combat fatigue: Disabling physical and emotional reaction incident to military combat. Paradoxically, the reaction may not necessarily include fatigue. Term especially common in World War II. Now replaced by combat neurosis or war neurosis.

commitment: A legal process for admitting a mentally ill person to a mental hospital. The legal definition and procedure vary from state to state. Typically requires a court or judicial procedure, although not in all states. Sometimes the commitment may be entirely voluntary.

communication, privileged: See *privilege.*

community mental health center: A health service delivery system first authorized by the federal Mental Retardation Facilities and Community Mental Health Centers Construction Act of 1963, to provide a coordinated program of continuing mental health care to a specific population. The CMHC is typically a community or neighborhood facility, or a network of affiliated agencies, that serves as a locus for the delivery of the various services included in the concept of *community psychiatry.* Emphasis is on provision of a comprehensive range of services and continuity of care that are readily accessible to the population served. Since 1964, regulations governing federal support for the centers have required that they offer at least five services, namely, inpatient, outpatient, partial hospitalization, emergency services, and consultation and education for community agencies. It is also considered desirable that the center should provide diagnostic, rehabilitative, precare and aftercare services, training, research, and public education.

The form and style of a center, and the specific programs it provides, are largely determined by the needs of the population it serves. Since emotional and mental health needs are so closely interwoven with broader social and political issues, centers serving different populations develop different ways of functioning. In some, for example, the emphasis will be on support services such as welfare, legal aid, placement and homemaker services. In others, the emphasis may be on alternatives to 24-hour inpatient care, such as day, night or weekend hospital, or day-care programs, drop-in lounges, outreach and home visits. Still others may lean heavily on *sociotherapy* with peer group interaction, indigenous workers and community caregivers in a storefront or similar non-clinical setting, or community socialization opportunities. See *caregiver, partial hospitalization.*

community psychiatry: That branch of *psychiatry* concerned with the provision and delivery of a coordinated program of mental health care to a specified population (usually all residents of a designated geographical area termed the *catchment area*). Implicit in the concept of community psychiatry is acceptance of continuing responsibility for all the mental health needs of the community— diagnosis, treatment, rehabilitation (tertiary *prevention*) and aftercare, and, equally important, early case-finding (secondary prevention), and promoting mental health and preventing psychosocial disorder (primary prevention). The organizational nucleus for such services is typically the *community mental health center.* The body of knowledge and theory on which the methods and techniques of community psychiatry are based is often called *social psychiatry.* See also *prevention.*

compensation: A *defense mechanism,* operating *unconsciously,* by which the individual attempts to make up for (i.e. to compensate for) real or fancied deficiencies. Also, a *conscious* process in which the individual strives to make up for real or imagined defects

34

of physique, performance, skills, or psychological attributes. The two types frequently merge.

compensation neurosis: An unofficial term for certain *unconscious* neurotic reactions in which features of *secondary gain* such as a situational or financial advantage, are prominent. To be distinguished from *malingering* where there is *conscious* concealment or an ulterior motive to defraud. See also *hysterical neurosis, conversion type,* under *neurosis.*

competency to stand trial: See *Table of Legal Terms,* p. 70.

complex: A group of associated ideas that have a common strong emotional tone. These are largely *unconscious* and significantly influence attitudes and associations. See also *castration complex, inferiority complex,* and *Oedipus complex.*

compression: The exertion of pressure on the brain, spinal cord, or nerve fibers by such conditions as fractures, blood clots, tumors, and abscesses.

compulsion: An insistent, repetitive, intrusive, and unwanted urge to perform an act that is contrary to the person's ordinary wishes or standards. Since it serves as a defensive substitute for still more unacceptable *unconscious* ideas and wishes, failure to perform the compulsive act leads to overt *anxiety.* Compulsions are *obsessions* that are still felt as *impulses.*

compulsive personality: A personality characterized by excessive adherence to rigid standards. Typically, the individual is inflexible, overconscientious, overinhibited, unable to relax, and exhibits repetitive patterns of behavior. See *obsessive compulsive personality* under *personality disorder.*

conative: Pertains to the basic strivings of an individual as expressed in his behavior and actions; volitional as contrasted with *cognitive.*

concordance: See *Table of Research Terms,* p. 74.

concussion: An impairment of brain function due to injury caused by a blow to the head. The speed and degree of recovery depend on severity of the brain injury. Symptoms may include headache, disorientation, paralysis, and occasionally unconsciousness.

condensation: A psychologic process often present in dreams in which two or more concepts are fused so that a single symbol represents the multiple components.

conditioned reinforcer: See *reinforcement* under *behavior therapy*.

conditioned stimulus: See *stimulus control* under *behavior therapy*.

conditioning: See under *behavior therapy*.

conditioning therapy: See under *behavior therapy*.

confabulation: See *Table of Neurologic Deficits*, p. 72.

confidentiality: The ethical principle that a physician may not reveal any information related to him in the course of medical attendance. See *privilege, privileged communication,* in *Table of Legal Terms*, p. 70.

conflict: A mental struggle that arises from the simultaneous operation of opposing *impulses, drives,* or external (environmental) or internal demands; termed *intrapsychic* when the conflict is between forces within the personality, *extrapsychic* when it is between the self and the environment.

confusion: Disturbed orientation in respect to time, place, or person. See *delirium, dementia, mental status, organic brain syndrome.*

congenital: Literally, present at birth. It may include conditions that arise during fetal development or with the birth process as well as hereditary or genetically determined conditions. It does not refer to conditions that appear after birth.

conscience: The morally self-critical part of the self-encompassing standards of behavior, performance, and value judgments. Commonly equated with the *superego*.

conscious: That part of the mind or mental functioning of which the content is subject to awareness or known to the person. In neurology: awake, alert. Contrast with *unconscious*.

constitution: A person's intrinsic physical and psychological endowment; sometimes used more narrowly to indicate the physical inheritance or potential from birth.

constitutional types: Constellations of morphologic, physiologic, and psychologic traits as earlier proposed by various scholars. Galen: sanguine, melancholic, choleric, and phlegmatic types; Kretschmer: pyknic (stocky), asthenic (slender), athletic, and dysplastic (disproportioned) types; Sheldon: ectomorphic (thin), mesomorphic (muscular), and endormorphic (fat) types, based on the relative preponderance of outer, middle, or inner layers of embryonic cellular tissue.

control group: See *Table of Research Terms,* p. 74.

conversion: A *defense mechanism,* operating *unconsciously,* by which intrapsychic *conflicts* that would otherwise give rise to *anxiety* are, instead, given symbolic external expression. The repressed ideas or impulses, plus the psychologic *defenses* against them, are converted into a variety of somatic symptoms. The symptoms may include such things as paralysis of a limb that prevents its use for aggressive purposes, pain, and loss of sensory function.

convulsive disorders: Primarily the centrencephalic seizures, grand mal and petit mal, and the focal seizures of Jacksonian and psychomotor *epilepsy.* These brain disorders, with their characteristic *electroencephalographic* patterns, are to be differentiated from a variety of other pathophysiological conditions in which a convulsive seizure may occur. For example, seizures may follow withdrawal from alcohol, barbiturates, and a wide variety of other drugs; they may also occur in *cerebral vascular disease,* brain tumor, brain abscess, *hypoglycemia,* hyponatremia, high fevers, eclampsia, uremia, and many other metabolic and intracranial disorders. Finally, hysterical seizures and seizures simulated by *malingerers* may, at times, pose difficult diagnostic problems in differentiation.

coping mechanisms: Ways of adjusting to environmental stress without altering one's goals or purposes; includes both *conscious* and *unconscious* mechanisms.

coprophagia: Eating of filth or feces.

coprophilia: Excessive or morbid interest in filth or feces or their symbolic representations.

37

core gender identity: See *gender identity*.

correlation: See *Table of Research Terms*, p. 74.

counterphobia: The desire or seeking out of experiences that are *consciously* or *unconsciously* feared.

countertransference: The psychiatrist's partly *unconscious* or *conscious* emotional reaction to his patient. See also *transference*.

couples therapy: See *marital counseling*.

cretinism: A type of *mental retardation* and body malformation caused by severe uncorrected thyroid deficiency in infancy and early childhood.

cri-du-chat: Chromosomal irregularity causing *mental retardation*. The name is derived from a cat-like cry emitted by children with this disorder. Piercing noises may be attributed to laryngeal abnormality. First described by Lejeune in 1963.

criminal responsibility: See *Table of Legal Terms*, p. 70.

crisis intervention: See *community psychiatry*.

cross-cultural psychiatry: The comparative study of mental illness and mental health among different societies, nations, and cultures. The latter term is often used synonomously with transcultural psychiatry, the "trans" prefix denoting that the vista of the scientific observer extends beyond the scope of a single cultural unit.

cultural anthropology: The study of man and his works, or of the learned behavior of man: his technology, languages, religions, values, customs, mores, beliefs, social relationships, and family life and structure. Originally restricting its studies to primitive or preliterate societies and to non-occidental civilized societies, cultural anthropology in recent years has enlarged its scope of interest to include studies of contemporary Western cultures. Of particular interest to psychiatry is the finding that what is considered as *psychopathological* is a matter of consensus within a given society. Similar to *social anthropology* and *ethnology*.

38

cultural psychiatry: A branch of *social psychiatry* that concerns itself with the mentally ill in relation to their cultural environment. Symptoms of behavior regarded as quite evident *psychopathology* in one society may well be regarded as acceptable and normal in another society.

culture specific syndromes: Forms of disturbed behavior that are highly specific to certain cultural systems and do not conform to Western *nosologic* entities. Commonly cited examples follow:

Syndrome	*Culture*	*Symptoms*
amok	Malay	Acute homicidal *mania*, screaming, attacks on people and inanimate objects.
koro	Chinese, S.E. Asia	Fear of death, fear of retraction of penis into abdomen, *anxiety*.
latah	S.E. Asia	Hypersuggestibility, *echolalia*, disorganization, automatic obedience.
piblokto	Eskimo women	Attacks of screaming, crying, and running naked through the snow, sometimes with suicidal or homicidal tendencies.
susto	Latin America	*Panic* reactions due to fear of the evil eye, black magic, and spirit possession.
windigo	Canadian Indians	*Delusions* of being possessed by a cannibalistic monster (windigo), attacks of agitated *depression*, oral *sadistic* fears and impulses.

cunnilingus: Sexual activity in which the mouth and tongue are used to stimulate female genitals. Within the range of normal sexual expression.

CVA: *Cerebrovascular accident.* See *stroke.*

cybernetics: Term introduced by Norbert Wiener (1894-1964) to designate the science of control mechanisms. It covers the field of communication and control of machines and puts forth the hypothesis that there is some similarity between the human nervous system and electronic control devices.

cyclothymic personality: See *personality disorders.*

D

day hospital: See *partial hospitalization*.

death instinct (Thanatos): In Freudian theory, the *unconscious drive* toward dissolution and death. Coexists with and is in opposition to the life *instinct* (Eros).

decompensation: The deterioration of existing *defenses*, leading to an exacerbation of pathological behavior.

defense mechanism: *Unconscious intrapsychic* processes serving to provide relief from emotional *conflict* and *anxiety*. *Conscious* efforts are frequently made for the same reasons, but true defense mechanisms are *unconscious*. Some of the common defense mechanisms defined in this glossary are: *compensation, conversion, denial, displacement, dissociation, idealization, identification, incorporation, introjection, projection, rationalization, reaction formation, regression, sublimation, substitution, symbolization, undoing*. See *mental mechanism*.

déjà vu: The sensation that what one is seeing one has seen before.

delirium: An acute reversible mental state characterized by confusion and altered, possibly fluctuating consciousness due to an alteration of cerebral metabolism with *delusions, illusions,* and/or *hallucinations*. Often emotional *lability*, typically appearing as *anxiety* and *agitation*, is present. Contrast with *dementia*. See also *organic brain syndrome*.

delirium tremens: An acute and sometimes fatal brain disorder (in 10–15% of untreated cases) caused by withdrawal or relative withdrawal from alcohol, usually developing in 24–96 hours. A history of excessive and unusually prolonged intake is present and the symptoms of the syndrome include fever, tremors, ataxia and sometimes *convulsions*, frightening *illusions*, *delusions*, and *hallucinations*. The condition is often accompanied by nutritional deficiencies. It is a medical emergency. Contrast with *alcoholic hallucinosis*. See also *Wernicke-Korsakoff syndrome*.

delusion: A firm, fixed idea not amenable to rational explanation. Maintained against logical argument despite objective contradictory evidence. Common delusions include:

> **delusions of grandeur:** Exaggerated ideas of one's importance or identity.
> **delusions of persecution:** Ideas that one has been singled out for persecution. See also *paranoia*.
> **delusions of reference:** Incorrect assumption that certain casual or unrelated events or the behavior of others apply to oneself. See also *paranoia*.

demand characteristics ("experimenter effects"): See *Table of Research Terms*, p. 74.

dementia: An irreversible mental state characterized by decreased intellectual function, personality change, impairment of judgment, and often changes in *affect*. It is due to permanently altered cerebral metabolism. Contrast with *delirium*. See *organic brain syndrome*.

dementia praecox: Obsolete descriptive term for *schizophrenia*. Introduced by Morel (1860) and later popularized by *Kraepelin*.

dementia, senile: See *senile dementia*.

denial: A *defense mechanism*, operating *unconsciously*, used to resolve emotional *conflict* and allay *anxiety* by disavowing thoughts, feelings, wishes, needs, or external reality factors that are *consciously* intolerable.

dependency needs: Vital needs for mothering, love, affection, shelter, protection, security, food, and warmth. May be a manifestation of *regression* when they reappear openly in adults.

41

depersonalization: Feelings of unreality or strangeness concerning either the environment or the self or both. See also *neurosis.*

depersonalization neurosis: See under *neurosis.*

depression: When used to describe mood, depression refers to feelings of sadness, despair and unhappiness. As such, depression is universally experienced and is a normal feeling state. The overt manifestations of depression are highly variable and may be *culture specific.*

Depression may also be a specific psychiatric diagnosis or component of illness. Slowed thinking and decreased purposeful physical activity accompany the mood change when the term is used diagnostically.

A number of types of depression are recognized. The *depressive neuroses* and *psychotic depressive reactions* occur in response to a precipitating event which may include a loss or threatened loss of loved persons or objects, or internal conflict. The *psychotic depressive reaction* is distinguished by severe functional impairment and by a loss of reality testing with regard to one's circumstances. Signs of depression may vary in different age groups. In children, manifestations of depression may include *regression, obsessive compulsive* symptoms, *acting out* behavior and the development of somatic complaints.

The major affective disorders, which include *manic-depressive psychosis* and *involutional melancholia,* are not readily attributable to a specific loss or stress and the depression is of a psychotic nature. Specific symptomatology which may accompany depressions includes: *agitation,* somatic preoccupations, sleep disturbances, appetite disturbances, *delusions* and *hallucinations,* and suicidal ideation and activity. The symptoms are considered due to the mood disorder rather than other *psychopathologic* processes such as *schizophrenia, alcoholism* or metabolic processes such as hormonal disturbances.

depressive neurosis: See *depression.*

deprivation, emotional: A lack of adequate and appropriate interpersonal and/or environmental experience, usually in the early developmental years.

deprivation, sensory: See *sensory deprivation.*

42

depth psychology: The psychology of *unconscious* mental processes. Also a system of psychology in which the study of such processes plays a major role, as in *psychoanalysis*.

dereistic: Describes mental activity that is not in accordance with reality, logic, or experience. Similar to autistic. See *autism*.

descriptive psychiatry: A system of psychiatry based upon the study of readily observable external factors; to be differentiated from *dynamic psychiatry*. Often used to refer to the systematized descriptions of mental illnesses formulated by *Kraepelin*.

desensitization: See under *behavior therapy*.

desoxyribonucleic acid (DNA): One of the key chemicals governing life functions. Found in the cell nucleus. Essential constituent of the *genes*. Governs the manufacture of *RNA*.

deterioration: Worsening of a clinical condition, usually expressed as progressive impairment of function. See *dementia, organic brain syndrome*. Contrast with *regression*.

determinism: The postulate that nothing in the individual's emotional life results from chance alone but rather from specific causes or forces known or unknown.

detoxification: Treatment by the use of medication, diet, rest, fluids, and nursing care to restore physiological functioning after it has been seriously disturbed by the overuse of alcohol, barbiturates, or other *addictive* drugs.

developmental disability: A disability which originates before the age of 18, which may be expected to continue indefinitely, and which constitutes a substantial handicap to an individual. The disability is attributable to *mental retardation*, cerebral palsy, *epilepsy*, or other neurologic conditions and includes *autism* when it is found to be closely related to mental retardation and to require treatment similar to that required for mentally retarded individuals.

differential reinforcement: See *reinforcement* under *behavior therapy*.

43

dipsomania: See *mania.*

disability (psychiatric): Deprivation of intellectual or emotional capacity or fitness. As defined by the federal government: "Inability to engage in any substantial gainful activity by reason of any medically determinable physical or mental impairment which can be expected to last or has lasted for a continuous period of not less than 12 full months." See also *developmental disability.*

discordance: See *Table of Research Terms,* p. 74.

discrimination: See *stimulus control* under *behavior therapy.*

discriminative stimulus: See *stimulus control* under *behavior therapy.*

disorientation: Loss of awareness of the position of the self in relation to space, time, or other persons; confusion. See *delirium, dementia.*

displacement: A *defense mechanism,* operating *unconsciously,* in which an *emotion* is transferred from its original object to a more acceptable substitute used to allay *anxiety.*

dissociation: A *defense mechanism,* operating *unconsciously,* through which emotional significance and *affect* are separated and detached from an idea, situation, or object. Dissociation may defer or postpone experiencing some emotional impact as, for example, in selective *amnesia.*

dissociative reaction: Same as *hysterical neurosis, dissociative type.* See *neurosis.*

distractibility: Inability to maintain attention, which is diverted from one area or topic to another in rapid shifts, with minimal provocation. Distractibility may be a manifestation of organic impairment, or it may be a part of functional disorders such as *anxiety* states, *mania,* or *schizophrenia.*

distributive analysis and synthesis: The therapy used by the psychobiologic school of psychiatry developed by Adolf *Meyer.* Entails extensive guided and directed investigation and analysis of the patient's entire past experience, stressing his assets and liabilities to make possible a constructive synthesis. See *psychobiology.*

Dix, Dorothea Lynde (1802–1887): Foremost nineteenth century American crusader for the improvement of institutional care of the mentally ill.

DNA: See *desoxyribonucleic acid.*

dominance: An individual's disposition to play a prominent or controlling role in his interaction with others. In neurology, the (normal) tendency of one half of the brain to be more important than the other in mediating various functions (cerebral dominance). In genetics, the ability of one *gene* (dominant gene) to express itself in the *phenotype* of an individual, even though that gene is paired with another (recessive gene) that would have expressed itself in a different way.

dopamine: A *catecholamine.* See *biogenic amines.*

double bind: A type of interaction in which one person demands a response to a message containing mutually contradictory signals while the other is unable either to comment on the incongruity or to escape from the situation. Felt by some to be a characteristic mode of interaction in families with a *schizophrenic* member. Example: a mother tells her son to act like a man and express his opinion and when he does, berates him as unloving and disloyal.

double-blind: See *Table of Research Terms,* p. 74.

double personality: See *personality, multiple.*

Down's syndrome: Preferred term for a common form of *mental retardation* caused by a *chromosomal* abnormality; formerly called mongolism. Two types are recognized based on the nature of the chromosomal aberration. The translocation type is due to a transmitted chromosomal abnormality and there is about a 15% likelihood that a subsequent child will also have the disorder if the mother is a carrier. Men can also be translocation carriers but produce a very low incidence of Down's syndrome babies (1%). The nondisjunction type is due to a chance disruption of chromosomes which occurs with increasing frequency as the woman ages. The likelihood of a subsequent pregnancy yielding a child with Down's syndrome in this situation is about the same as it is for other women of the same age. The *incidence* is very low in younger

45

women but rises to about one in fifty by age 45. Physical findings of greatest frequency include: widely spaced eyes with slanting openings, small head with flattened occiput, lax joints, flabby hands, and small ears. *Congenital* anomalies of the heart are common.

Draw-a-Person (Family, House, Tree): See *Table of Psychological Tests*, p. 78.

drive: Basic urge, instinct, motivation; a term currently preferred to avoid confusion with the more purely biological concept of *instinct*.

drug abuse: See under *drug dependence*.

drug dependence: Habituation to, abuse of, and/or *addiction* to a chemical substance. Largely because of psychologic craving, the life of the drug-dependent person revolves about his need for the specific effect of one or more chemical agents on his mood or state of consciousness. The term thus includes not only addiction, (which emphasizes physiologic dependence), but also drug abuse, (where the pathologic craving for drugs seems unrelated to physical dependence). Examples: alcohol; opiates; synthetic analgesics with morphine-like effects; barbiturates, other hypnotics, sedatives, and some antianxiety agents; cocaine; psychostimulants; marijuana; and *psychotomimetic* drugs.

drug holiday: Discontinuing the administration of a drug for a limited period of time in order to evaluate baseline behavior and to control the dosage of psychoactive drugs and side effects.

drug interaction: The effects of two or more drugs being taken simultaneously producing an alteration in the usual effects of either drug taken alone. The interacting drugs may have a potentiating or additive effect and serious side effects may result. An example of drug interaction is alcohol and sedative drugs taken together which may cause additive *central nervous system* depression.

DSM-I: Refers to the first edition of the American Psychiatric Association's *Diagnostic and Statistical Manual of Mental Disorders* published in 1952. It was superseded by the second edition (*DSM II*) published in 1968.

46

DSM-II: Abbreviation for *Diagnostic and Statistical Manual of Mental Disorders,* Second Edition (1968).

dummy: British term for *placebo.*

Durham Rule: See *Table of Legal Terms,* p. 70.

dyadic: The therapeutic relationship between doctor and one patient as in individual *psychotherapy.*

dynamic psychiatry: As distinguished from *descriptive psychiatry* refers to the study of emotional processes, their origins, and the mental mechanisms. Implies the study of the active, energy laden, and changing factors in human behavior and their motivation. Dynamic principles convey the concepts of change, of evolution, and of progression or *regression.*

dynamics: See *psychodynamics.*

dys: See *Table of Neurologic Deficits,* p. 72.

dysarthria: See *Table of Neurologic Deficits,* p. 72.

dyscalculia: See *learning disability.*

dysgeusia: See *Table of Neurologic Deficits,* p. 72.

dysgraphia: See *learning disability.*

dyslexia: Inability or difficulty in reading, including word-blindness and strephosymbolia (tendency to reverse letters and words in reading and writing), See *learning disability* and also *alexia* in *Table of Neurologic Deficits,* p. 72.

dysmnesia, dysmnesic syndrome: General intellectual impairment secondary to defects of memory and orientation; see *organic brain syndrome.*

dyspareunia: Painful sexual intercourse in the woman.

dysphagia: Difficult or painful swallowing.

dysphoria: Disorder of mood.

dyssocial behavior: A diagnostic term for individuals who are not classifiable as *anti-social personalities*, but who are predatory and follow more or less criminal pursuits. Formerly called "sociopathic personalities."

E

early infantile autism: A *syndrome* considered to be a primary problem which begins in infancy and is characterized by self-absorption, inaccessibility, and failure to develop attachment to a mother figure. There is a preoccupation with inanimate objects, desire for sameness in the environment and general disturbance of function.

echolalia: See *Table of Neurologic Deficits*, p. 72.

echopraxia: The pathologic repetition, by imitation, of the movements of another. Sometimes seen in *schizophrenia, catatonic type*.

ecology: Study of relations between organisms and their environments, especially the study of relations among human beings, their environment, and human institutions.

ECT (electroconvulsive treatment): See *shock treatment*.

ectomorphic: See *constitutional types*.

educable: See *mental retardation*.

EEG: See *electroencephalogram*.

ego: In *psychoanalytic* theory, one of the three major divisions in the model of the psychic apparatus, the others being the *id* and *superego.* The ego represents the sum of certain *mental mechanisms,* such as perception and memory, and specific *defense mechanisms.* The ego serves to mediate between the demands of primitive instinctual *drives* (the *id*), of internalized parental and social prohibitions (the *superego*) , and of reality. The compromises between these forces achieved by the ego tend to resolve intrapsychic *conflict* and serve an adaptive and executive function. Psychiatric usage of the term should not be confused with common usage, which connotes "self-love" or "selfishness."

ego alien: See *ego-dystonic.*

ego analysis: Intensive psychoanalytic study and analysis of the ways in which the *ego* resolves or attempts to deal with intrapsychic *conflicts,* especially in relation to the development of *mental mechanisms* and the maturation of capacity for rational thought and action. Modern *psychoanalysis* gives more emphasis to considerations of the defensive operations of the ego than did earlier techniques, which emphasized *instinctual* forces to a greater degree.

ego-dystonic: Aspects of the individual's behavior, thoughts, and attitudes that he views as repugnant or inconsistent with his total personality. See also *ego-syntonic.*

ego ideal: That part of the *personality* that comprises the aims and goals of the self; usually refers to the *conscious* or *unconscious* emulation of significant figures with whom the person has identified. The ego ideal emphasizes what one should be or do in contrast to what one should not be or do.

egomania: See under *-mania.*

ego-syntonic: Aspects of the individual's behavior, thoughts, and attitudes that he views as acceptable and consistent with his total personality. See also *ego-dystonic.*

eidetic image: Unusually vivid and apparently exact mental image; may be a memory, fantasy, or dream.

ejaculatory incompetence (impotence): Inability to reach *orgasm* and ejaculate during sexual intercourse in spite of adequacy of erection.

elaboration: An *unconscious* process of expansion and embellishment

49

of detail, especially with reference to a symbol or representation in a dream.

Electra complex: An infrequently used term describing the pathological relationship of a woman with men based on unresolved developmental *conflicts* partially analogous to the *Oedipus complex* in the man.

electroconvulsive treatment (ECT): See *shock treatment.*

electroencephalogram (EEG): A graphic (voltage vs time) depiction of the brain's electrical potentials, recorded by scalp electrodes. It is used for diagnosis in neurological and neuropsychiatric disorders and in neurophysiological research. Sometimes used interchangeably with electrocorticogram and depth record, where the electrodes are in direct contact with brain tissue.

electromyogram (EMG): An electrophysiological recording made of muscle potentials which gives a measure of the amount and nature of muscle activity at the site from which the recording is taken. It may be used in *biofeedback* treatment of conditions such as tension headache.

electroshock treatment (EST): See *electroconvulsive treatment* under *shock treatment.*

electrosleep: Original name for *cerebral electrotherapy (CET).* A literal translation from the Russian. Misleading as the treatment does not induce sleep.

electrostimulation: See *electroconvulsive treatment* under *shock treatment.*

electrotherapy: See *cerebral electrotherapy (CET).*

eliciting stimulus: See *stimulus control* under *behavior therapy.*

elopement: A patient's unauthorized departure from a mental hospital or facility.

emancipated minor: See *Table of Legal Terms,* p. 70.

EMG: See *electromyogram.*

emotion: A feeling such as fear, anger, grief, joy or love which may not always be *conscious.* See also *affect.*

emotional disturbance: See *mental disorder.*

emotional health: See *mental health.*

emotional illness: See *mental disorder.*

empathy: An objective and insightful awareness of the feelings, *emotions* and behavior of another person, their meaning and significance; usually subjective and noncritical. Contrast with *sympathy.*

encephalitis: Inflammation of the brain which may be acute or chronic, caused by viruses, bacteria, spirochetes, fungi, protozoa, and chemicals (such as lead). Neurological signs and symptoms and various mental and behavioral changes occur during the illness and may persist. See *encephalopathy, organic brain syndromes.*

encephalopathy: A broad term designating any of the metabolic, toxic, neoplastic, or degenerative diseases of the brain.

encopresis: Incontinence of feces.

encounter group: A *sensitivity group* stressing emotional rather than intellectual insight. It is oriented to the here and now, with the emphasis on developing awareness through confrontation to improve coping behavior.

endemic: See under *epidemiology.*

endocrine disorders: Disturbances of the function of the ductless glands which may be metabolic in origin and may be associated with or aggravated by emotional factors producing mental and behavioral disturbances in addition to physical signs.

endogenous psychoses: See *organic brain syndrome.*

endomorphic: See *constitutional types.*

engram: A memory trace. Theoretically, a change in neural tissue that accounts for persistence of memory.

enuresis: Incontinence of urine. See *Table of Sleep Disorders,* p. 84.

epidemiology: The study of the incidence, distribution, prevalence, and control of *mental disorders* in a given population. Common terms used in epidemiology are:

51

endemic: Describes a disorder that is native to or restricted to a particular area.

epidemic: Describes a disorder or the outbreak of a disorder that affects significant numbers of persons in a given population at any time.

pandemic: Describes a disorder that occurs over a very wide area or in many countries, or even universally.

See also *incidence, point* and *period prevalence* in *Table of Research Terms,* p. 74.

epilepsy: A disorder characterized by periodic motor or sensory seizures or their equivalents, and sometimes accompanied by a loss of consciousness or by certain equivalent manifestations. May be idiopathic (no known organic cause) or symptomatic (due to organic lesions). Accompanied by abnormal electrical discharge which may be shown by *EEG*. See *convulsive disorders*.

> **epileptic equivalent:** Episodic, sensory, or motor phenomena which an individual with epilepsy may experience instead of convulsive seizures.
>
> **Jacksonian epilepsy:** Recurrent episodes of convulsive seizures or spasms without loss of consciousness localized in a part or region of the body. Named after J. Hughlings Jackson (1835–1911).
>
> **major epilepsy (grand mal):** Characterized by gross convulsive seizures with loss of consciousness and vegetative control.
>
> **minor epilepsy (petit mal):** Minor, non-convulsive epileptic seizures or equivalents; may be limited only to momentary lapses of consciousness.
>
> **psychomotor epilepsy:** Recurrent periodic disturbances, usually originating in the temporal lobes, of behavior during which the patient carries out movements that are often repetitive, highly organized but semiautomatic in character.

epinephrine: One of the *catecholamines* secreted by the adrenal gland and by fibers of the *sympathetic nervous system*. It is responsible for many of the physical manifestations of *fear* and *anxiety*. Also known as adrenalin.

Erikson, Erik H. (1902–): German born lay *psychoanalyst* and child psychoanalyst; author of major psychodynamic studies of

Luther and Ghandi, and noted for his work on *psychosocial development.*

erogenous zone: See *erotogenic zone.*

erotic: *Consciously* or *unconsciously* invested with sexual feeling; sensually related.

erotogenic zone: An area of the body particularly susceptible to *erotic* arousal when stimulated, especially the oral, anal, and genital areas. Sometimes called erogenous zone.

erotomania: See *-mania.*

erythrophobia: See under *phobia.*

ESP: See *extrasensory perception.*

EST (also ECT): See *electroconvulsive treatment* under *shock treatment.*

ethology: The scientific study of animal behavior. Also the empirical study of human behavior.

etiology: Causation, particularly with reference to disease.

euphoria: An exaggerated feeling of physical and emotional well-being not consonant with apparent stimuli or events; usually of psychologic origin, but also seen in organic brain disease, toxic, and drug induced states. See *manic depressive psychosis.*

executive ego function: A *psychoanalytic* term for the ego's management of the *mental mechanisms* in order to meet the needs of the organism. See also *ego.*

exhibitionism: A man exposing his genitals to women or girls in socially unacceptable situations. See *sexual deviation.*

existential psychiatry (existentialism): A school of psychiatry evolved from orthodox *psychoanalytic* thought. Stresses the way in which man experiences the phenomenological world about him and takes responsibility for his existence. Philosophically, it is *holistic* and self-deterministic in contrast to biologically or culturally deterministic points of view. See *phenomenology* and *Table of Schools of Psychiatry*, p. 77.

53

exogenous psychoses: See *organic brain syndrome.*

experimental study designs: See *Table of Research Terms*, p. 74.

explosive personality: See *personality disorders.*

extinction: See *reinforcement* under *behavior therapy.*

extrapsychic: That which takes place between the *psyche* (mind) and the environment.

extrapsychic conflict: See under *conflict.*

extrapyramidal syndrome: A variety of signs and symptoms including muscular rigidity, tremors, drooling, restlessness, peculiar involuntary movements and postures, shuffling gait, protrusion of the tongue, chewing movements, blurred vision, and many other neurological disturbances. Results from dysfunction of the *extrapyramidal system.* May occur as a reversible side effect of certain psychotropic drugs, particularly *phenothiazines.* See *Parkinson's disease, tardive dyskinesia, dyskinetic syndromes,* and *Table of Neurologic Deficits*, p. 72.

extrapyramidal system: The portion of the *central nervous system* responsible for coordinating and integrating various aspects of motor behavior or bodily movements.

extrasensory perception (ESP): Perception without recourse to the conventional use of any of the five physical senses. See also *telepathy.*

extraversion: A state in which attention and energies are largely directed outward from the self, as opposed to inward toward the self, as in *introversion.*

F

falsifiable hypothesis: See *Table of Research Terms,* p. 74.

family therapy: Treatment of more than one member of the family simultaneously in the same session. The treatment may be supportive, directive, or interpretive. The assumption is that a mental disorder in one member of a family may be a manifestation of disorder in other members and may affect their interrelationships and functioning.

fantasy: An imagined sequence of events or mental images, e.g., day dreams. Serves to express *unconscious conflicts,* to gratify unconscious wishes, or to prepare for anticipated future events.

fear: Emotional and physiologic response to recognized sources of danger, to be distinguished from *anxiety.* See *phobia.*

feeblemindedness: Obsolete term. See *mental retardation.*

fellatio: Sexual stimulation of the penis by oral contact; within the range of normal sexual expression.

femaleness: Anatomic and physiologic features which relate to the female's procreative and nurturant capacities. See also *feminine.*

feminine: An adjective to describe a set of sex-specific social role behaviors that are unrelated to procreative and nurturant biologic function. See also *gender identity, gender role,* and *femaleness.*

fetishism: A *sexual deviation* characterized by attachment of special meaning to an inanimate object (or fetish) which serves, usually

55

unconsciously, as a substitute for the original object or person. The fetish is essential for completion of orgasm. Rare in females.

fixation: The arrest of psychosexual maturation. Depending on degree it may be either normal or pathological. See *psychosexual development*.

flagellation: A *masochistic* or *sadistic* act in which one or both participants derive stimulation, usually *erotic*, from whipping or being whipped.

flexibilitas cerea: See *cerea flexibilitas*.

flight of ideas: Verbal skipping from one idea to another. The ideas appear to be continuous but are fragmentary and determined by chance or temporal associations. Sometimes seen in *manic-depressive psychosis*.

flooding: See under *behavior therapy*.

folie à deux: A condition in which two closely related persons, usually in the same family, share the same *delusions*.

Food and Drug Administration (FDA): One of six health administrations under the Assistant Secretary for Health of the U.S. Department of Health, Education and Welfare to set standards for, license the sale of, and in general to safeguard the public from the use of dangerous drugs and food substances.

forensic psychiatry: That branch of psychiatry dealing with legal issues related to mental disorders. See also *Table of Legal Terms*, p. 70.

foreplay: Sexual play preceding intercourse, usually pleasurable.

formication: The tactile *hallucination* or *illusion* that insects are crawling on the body or under the skin.

free association: In *psychoanalytic* therapy, spontaneous, uncensored verbalization by the patient of whatever comes to mind.

free floating anxiety: Severe, generalized, persisting *anxiety*, not specifically ascribed to a particular object or event and often a precusor of *panic*.

Freud, Anna (1895–   ): Austrian *psychoanalyst* and daughter of Sigmund *Freud*, noted for her contributions to the developmental theory of *psychoanalysis* and its application to preventive work with children.

Freud, Sigmund (1856–1939): Founder of *psychoanalysis*. Most of the basic concepts of *dynamic psychiatry* are derived from his theories.

frigidity: See *orgasmic impairment*.

Frostig Developmental Test of Visual Perception: See *Table of Psychological Tests*, p. 78.

fugue: Personality *dissociation* characterized by *amnesia*, and involving actual physical flight from the customary environment or field of *conflict*.

functional: In medicine, changes in the way an organ system operates that are not attributed to known structural alterations. See *functional disorder*.

functional disorder: A disorder in which the performance or operation of an organ or organ system is abnormal, but not as a result of known changes in structure.

G

galvanic skin response (GSR): The resistance of the skin to the passage of a weak electric current; an easily measured variable widely used in experimental studies as a measure of an individual's response to stimuli.

Ganser's syndrome: Sometimes called "nonsense syndrome" or "syndrome of approximate answers" or "prison psychosis" (e.g. "two times two equals about five"). Commonly used to characterize behavior of prisoners who seek—either *consciously* or *unconsciously*—to mislead others regarding their mental state in order to gain an advantage or escape responsibility.

Gault decision: See *Table of Legal Terms*, p. 70.

gegenhalten: See *Table of Neurologic Deficits*, p. 72.

gender identity (core gender identity): The inner sense of *maleness* or *femaleness* which identifies the person as being male, female or ambivalent. Gender identity differentiation takes place in infancy and very early childhood (up to about 30 months) through daily rearing practices of parental and other caring figures and is reinforced by the hormonal changes of puberty. Group values may cause conflicts about gender identity by labeling certain nonsexual interests and behavior as *masculine* or *feminine*. Gender identity is distinguished from sexual identity which is biologically determined. See also *gender role, transsexualism*.

gender role: The image the individual presents to others and to the self that declares him or her to be boy or girl, man or woman. Gender role is the public declaration of *gender identity* but the two do not necessarily coincide.

general paralysis (general paresis): An *organic brain syndrome* resulting from a chronic syphilitic infection. Occasionally associated with other neurological signs of syphilitic involvement of the nervous system. Detectable with laboratory tests of the blood or spinal fluid. Sometimes known as GPI (general paralysis of the insane), an obsolete term of historical interest.

general systems theory: A theoretical framework that views events from the standpoint of the "systems" involved in the event. Systems are groups of organized interacting components. The behavior of each system is determined by its own structure, by the aggregate characteristics of its component systems, and by the larger systems ("suprasystems") of which it is a component. Consequently, all systems may be viewed as part of an interrelated hierarchy (e.g. from subatomic particles to whole societies). The value of this theory in *psychiatry* lies in its emphasis on the *holistic* nature of *personality* (as compared to mechanistic, stimulus-response, and *cybernetic* theories, for example) and in its potential for advancing interdisciplinary understanding by integrating concepts about all of the systems, infrasystems, and suprasystems that affect human behavior.

generalization: See *stimulus control* under *behavior therapy*.

genes: The fundamental units of heredity. Composed of DNA (*desoxyribonucleic acid*) and arranged in a characteristic linear order on *chromosomes* within cell nuclei, they determine the *genotype* of the individual.

genetic: In biology, pertaining to *genes* or to inherited characteristics. Also, in *psychiatry*, pertaining to the historical development of an individual's psychological attributes or disorders.

genic: Referring to *genes*.

genital phase: See *psychosexual development*.

genotype: The total set of *genes* received by an individual at the time of conception, producing the genetic constitution. See *phenotype*.

geriatrics (geriatric psychiatry): A branch of medicine dealing with the aging process and diseases of the aging human. Geriatric psychiatry concerns itself with the psychological aspects of the aging process and *mental disorders* of the aged.

gerontology: The study of aging.

Gesell Developmental Schedules: See *Table of Psychological Tests*, p. 78.

Gestalt psychology: A German school of *psychology* that emphasizes a total perceptual configuration and the interrelations of its component parts. See *schools of psychiatry* and *Table of Schools of Psychiatry*, p. 77.

Gilles de la Tourette syndrome: A syndrome beginning in early childhood characterized by repetitive tics, other movement disorders, uncontrollable grunts and other unintelligible sounds, and occasionally verbal obscenities. Treatable with medications.

globus hystericus: An hysterical symptom in which there is a disturbing sensation of a lump in the throat. See also *hysterical neurosis, conversion type* under *neurosis.*

glossolalia: Gibberish speech.

grand mal: See *epilepsy.*

grandiose: Exaggerated belief or claims of one's importance or identity; often manifested by delusions of great wealth, power, or fame. See *manic depressive psychosis* and *mania.*

grief: Normal, appropriate emotional response to an external and *consciously* recognized loss; it is usually self-limited and gradually subsides within a reasonable time. To be distinguished from *depression.*

gross stress reaction: An acute emotional reaction incident to severe environmental stress as, for example, in industrial, domestic, civilian or military disasters, and other life situations.

group psychotherapy: Application of psychotherapeutic techniques to a group, including utilization of interactions of members of the group. Usually six to eight persons comprise a group and sessions typically last from 75-105 minutes. When performed by a psychiatrist, it is a form of medical psychotherapy.

groups: See *encounter group, marathon group, T-group, sensitivity group, group psychotherapy.*

H

habeas corpus: See *Table of Legal Terms,* p. 70.

halfway house: A specialized residence for patients who do not require full hospitalization but who need an intermediate degree of care before returning to independent community living. See also *community mental health center.*

hallucination: A false sensory perception in the absence of an actual external stimulus. May be induced by emotional and other factors such as drugs, alcohol, and *stress.* May occur in any of the senses.

hallucinogen: A chemical agent that produces *hallucinations.*

hallucinosis: A condition in which the patient hallucinates in a state of clear consciousness. See *alcoholic hallucinosis.*

haloperidol: See *Table of Drugs Used in Psychiatry,* p. 68.

health insurance: A generic term applying to all types of insurance indemnifying or reimbursing for costs of hospital and medical care or lost income arising from illness or injury. Approximately two-thirds of the population in the United States have some coverage of hospital care for mental conditions under private health insurance and about 38 percent have some coverage of outpatient psychiatric care.

health maintenance organization (HMO): A form of group practice by physicians and supporting personnel to provide comprehensive health services to an enrolled group of subscribers who pay a fixed premium to belong. The emphasis is on maintaining the health of the enrollees as well as treating their illnesses. HMOs should and often do include psychiatric services among their benefits.

hebephrenia: See *schizophrenia.*

hedonistic: Refers to pleasure seeking behavior. Contrast with *anhedonia.*

hermaphrodite: A person born with defective differentiation of sexual anatomic structures.

heuristic: See *Table of Research Terms,* p. 74.

histrionic: See *hysterical personality* under *personality disorders.*

HMO: See *health maintenance organization.*

holistic: An approach to the study of the individual in totality, rather than as an aggregate of separate physiological, *psychological,* and social characteristics.

61

homeostasis: Self-regulating biological processes which maintain the equilibrium of the organism. Referred to by Cannon and Johnson as "the wisdom of the body."

homosexual panic: An acute and severe attack of *anxiety* based upon *unconscious conflicts* involving *homosexuality*.

homosexuality: Sexual orientation towards persons of the same sex. Not a psychiatric disorder as such. See also *sexual orientation disturbance*.

Horney, Karen (1883–1952): German *psychoanalyst* who emigrated to the United States in 1932, departed from orthodox Freudian thought and founded her own school emphasizing cultural factors underlying the *neuroses*.

hot line: Telephone assistance for people in need of crisis intervention (e.g. suicide prevention), staffed by trained lay people with mental health professionals used in an advisory or back-up capacity; also serves a preventive function and as a line of communication between different community services. Most hot lines operate 24 hours a day, seven days a week. See also *community mental health center* and *community psychiatry*.

Huntington's disease (chorea): An hereditary and progressively degenerative disease of the *central nervous system* transmitted as an autosomal dominant trait. Onset is in adult life. Characterized by random movements (lurching, jerking) of the entire body, *psychosis*, and progressive mental deterioration.

hyperactivity (hyperkinesis): Increased or excessive muscular activity seen in diverse neurologic and psychiatric disorders.

hyperkinetic syndrome: A disorder of childhood or *adolescence* characterized by overactivity, restlessness, distractibility and short attention span. Difficulties in learning and perceptual motor function are found; in some cases believed to be associated with *minimal brain dysfunction*.

hypersomnia: See *Table of Sleep Disorders*, p. 84.

hyperventilation: Overbreathing associated with *anxiety* and marked by reduction of blood carbon dioxide, subjective complaints of light-headedness, faintness, tingling of the extremities, palpitations, and respiratory distress.

hypesthesia: A state of diminished sensitivity to tactile stimuli.

hypnagogic: Related to the semiconscious state immediately preceding sleep; sometimes also loosely used as equivalent to *hypnotic* or "sleep-inducing." See *Table of Sleep Disorders*, p. 84.

hypnagogic hallucinations: *Hallucinations* occurring during the *hypnagogic* state. Usually of no pathologic significance.

hypnosis: A state of increased receptivity to direction and suggestion, initially induced by the influence of another person. It is often characterized by an altered state of consciousness. The degree may vary from mild hypersuggestibility to a trance state with complete anesthesia.

hypnotherapy: See *hypnosis.*

hypnotic: Any agent that induces *sleep.* While *sedatives* and *narcotics* in sufficient dosage may produce sleep as an incidental effect, the term "hypnotic" is appropriately reserved for drugs employed primarily to produce sleep.

hypochondriacal neurosis: See under *neurosis.*

hypoglycemia: Abnormally low level of blood sugar. Thought by some to be a psychophysiological determinant of certain fatigue states.

hypomania: A psychopathological state and abnormality of mood falling somewhere between normal *euphoria* and *mania.* It is characterized by increased happiness, optimism, mild to moderate pressure of speech and activity, and a decrease in the need for sleep. Some individuals show increased creativity during hypomanic states, while others show signs of poor judgment, irritability and irascibility. See *manic depressive psychosis.*

hysterical neurosis: See under *neurosis.*

hysterical personality: See *personality disorders.*

63

hysterical psychosis: An unofficial term for an acute situational reaction in an histrionic type of person, usually manifested by the sudden onset of *hallucinations, delusions,* bizarre behavior, and volatile affect. As so defined, the term includes certain *culture specific syndromes* such as *amok, koro,* and *latah.*

hysterics: Lay term for uncontrollable emotional outbursts.

I

iatrogenic illness: An illness unwittingly precipitated, aggravated, or induced by the physician's attitude, examination, comments, or treatment.

ICD (ICD-8, ICDA): See *International Classification of Diseases.*

ICT (insulin coma treatment): See *shock treatment.*

id: In Freudian theory, that part of the personality structure which harbors the *unconscious instinctual* desires and strivings of the individual. See also *ego, superego.*

idealization: A *mental mechanism,* operating *consciously* or *unconsciously,* in which the individual overestimates an admired aspect or attribute of another person.

ideas of reference: Incorrect interpretation of casual incidents and external events as having direct reference to one's self. May reach sufficient intensity to constitute *delusions.*

idée fixe: Fixed idea. Used to describe a *compulsive* drive, an *obsessive* idea, or a *delusion.*

identification: A *defense mechanism,* operating *unconsciously,* by which an individual patterns himself after another. Identification plays a major role in the development of one's personality and specifically of the *superego.* To be differentiated from imitation, which is a *conscious* process.

identity crisis: A loss of the sense of the sameness and historical continuity of one's self, and inability to accept or adopt the role the subject perceives as being expected of him by society; often expressed by isolation, withdrawal, extremism, rebelliousness, and *negativity,* and typically triggered by a combination of sudden increase in the strength of instinctual *drives* in a milieu of rapid social evolution and technological change. See also *psychosocial development.*

idiopathic: Of unknown cause.

idiot: Obsolete term. See *mental retardation.*

idiot savant: An individual with gross *mental retardation* who nonetheless is capable of performing certain remarkable feats in sharply circumscribed intellectual areas such as calendar calculation and puzzle solving.

Illinois Test of Psycholinguistic Ability (ITPA): See *Table of Psychological Tests,* p. 78.

illusion: The misinterpretation of a real experience. Contrast with *hallucination.*

imago: In Jungian *psychology,* an *unconscious* mental image, usually idealized, of an important person in the early history of the individual.

imbecile: Obsolete term. See *mental retardation.*

implosion: See under *behavior therapy.*

impotence: The inability to achieve or maintain an erection of sufficient quality to engage in intercourse successfully. Two types are described by Masters and Johnson: in primary impotence there has never been a successful sexual coupling; in secondary impotence failure occurs following at least one successful union. Typically, secondary impotence occurs following an extended period of satis-factory functioning. An episode of secondary impotence is not unusual but assumes clinical significance when it becomes an established pattern of response.

imprinting: A term in *ethology* referring to a process similar to rapid learning or behavioral patterning that occurs at critical points in very early stages of development in animals. The extent to which imprinting occurs in human development has not been established.

impulse: A psychic striving; usually refers to an *instinctual* urge.

impulse disorders: An unofficial term for a varied group of nonpsy-chotic disorders in which impulse control is weak. The impulsive behavior is usually pleasurable, irresistible, and *ego-syntonic*.

inadequate personality: See *personality disorders*.

incidence: See *Table of Research Terms*, p. 74 and *epidemiology*.

incorporation: A primitive *defense mechanism*, operating *uncon-sciously*, in which the psychic representation of a person or parts of him, are figuratively ingested.

indigenous worker: See *caregiver*.

individual psychology: A system of psychiatric theory, research, and therapy developed by Alfred *Adler* which stresses *compensation* and *overcompensation* for inferiority feelings. See *complex*.

Indoklon treatment: See *shock treatment*.

indoles: A group of *biogenic amines*.

industrial psychiatry: See *occupational psychiatry*.

inferiority complex: See *complex*.

information theory: A system that deals with the mathematical characteristics of communicated messages and the systems that transmit, propagate, distort, or receive them.

infradian rhythms: See *biological rhythms*.

THE TABLES

TABLE OF DRUGS USED IN PSYCHIATRY

Generic Names	Trade Names (Examples)
ANTIANXIETY DRUGS	
Benzodiazepine Derivatives	
chlordiazepoxide	Librium
diazepam	Valium
oxazepam	Serax
Antihistaminic Derivatives	
hydroxyzine	Atarax, Vistaril
Sedative Types	
barbiturates (numerous types)	Numerous brands
meprobamate	Equanil, Miltown
tybamate	Solacen, Tybatran
ANTIDEPRESSANTS	
Tricyclic Derivatives	
amitriptyline	Elavil
desipramine	Norpramin, Pertofrane
doxepine	Sinequan, Adapin
imipramine	Tofranil, SK-Pramine, Imavate
nortriptyline	Aventyl
protriptyline	Vivactil
Hydrazide MAO Inhibitors	
isocarboxazid	Marplan
phenelzine	Nardil
Non-hydrazide MAO Inhibitors	
tranylcypromine	Parnate
Stimulants	
dextroamphetamine	Numerous brands
methamphetamine	Numerous brands
methylphenidate	Plimasin, Ritalin
ANTIMANIC DRUGS	
lithium carbonate	Eskalith, Lithane, Lithonate
chlorpromazine	Thorazine
haloperidol	Haldol
reserpine	Numerous brands

ANTIPSYCHOTIC DRUGS

Phenothiazine Derivatives
 Aliphatic
  chlorpromazine   Thorazine
  triflupromazine   Vesprin
 Piperidine
  thioridazine   Mellaril
  mesoridazine   Serentil
  piperacetazine   Quide
 Piperazine
  carphenazine   ———
  acetophenazine   Tindal
  prochlorperazine   Compazine
  thiopropazate   Dartal
  perphenazine   Trilafon
  butaperazine   Repoise
  trifluoperazine   Stelazine
  fluphenazine   Prolixin, Permitil
Thioxanthene Derivatives
  chlorprothixene   Taractan
  thiothixene   Navane
Butyrophenones
  haloperidol   Haldol
Dihydroindolones
  molindone   Mobane

TABLE OF LEGAL TERMS

care and protection proceedings: Intervention by a court on behalf of a child's health, education and welfare, when the parents or caretakers are unwilling or unable to provide it.

competency to stand trial: The test for competency to stand trial applies to the defendant's state of mind at the time of the trial. An individual is competent to stand trial when (1) he understands the nature of the charge he faces and the consequences that may result from his conviction, and (2) he is able to assist his attorney in his defense.

criminal responsibility: This applies to a defendant's state of mind at the time of the alleged crime. A person cannot be convicted of a crime if it can be proved that he lacked the ability to formulate a criminal intent at the time of the alleged crime because of "criminal insanity." See **insanity defense.**

emancipated minor: A minor who can be considered to have the rights of an adult when it can be shown that he or she is in fact exercising general control over his or her life.

Gault Decision: A landmark case which states that juvenile court proceedings must measure up to the essentials of due process and fair treatment under the 14th amendment. Namely, the juvenile must be (1) given proper notice of the charges, (2) represented by counsel, (3) protected against self-incrimination, and (4) able to confront and cross-examine witnesses.

habeas corpus: The legal term most commonly used to describe a petition which asks a court to decide whether confinement, of any sort, has been accomplished with due process of law.

insanity defense: A legal concept that a person cannot be convicted of a crime if he lacked **criminal responsibility** by reason of insanity, which term is defined as a matter of law. The premise is that where an alleged criminal lacks the **mens rea** because of insanity, such a person lacks criminal responsibility and cannot be convicted. Standards which the courts in Anglo-American law have established to define insanity have changed over the last century, and continue to change. The major landmark decisions defining insanity are:

> **M'Naghten Rule:** The English House of Lords in 1843 ruled that a person was not responsible for a crime if the accused "was laboring under such a defect of reason from disease of the mind as not to know the nature and quality of the act; or, if he did know it, that he did not know that what he was doing was wrong." This rule still obtains in most states.

> **irresistible impulse test:** The rule that a person is not responsible for a crime if he acts through an irresistible impulse which he was unable

to control because of a mental disease. Still accepted in some states, but rejected by most. Introduced in 1922.

Durham Rule: A ruling by the U.S. Court of Appeals for the District of Columbia in 1954 that held that "an accused is not criminally responsible if his unlawful act was the product of mental disease or mental defect." Since replaced in the District of Columbia by the **American Law Institute Formulation** following.

American Law Institute Formulation: Section 4.01 of the ALI's Model Penal Code states that "a person is not responsible for criminal conduct if at the time of such conduct as a result of mental disease or defect he lacks substantial capacity either to appreciate the wrongfulness of his conduct or to conform his conduct to the requirements of law." Adopted by the Second Circuit U.S. Court of Appeals in 1966 and by the U.S. Court of Appeals for the District of Columbia in 1972 (United States vs. Brawner).

mens rea: An intent to do harm. In a criminal case involving a defendant's mental state an important question may be whether or not he had mens rea, the ability to form an intention to do harm.

privilege: The legal right of a patient, always established by statute, to prevent his physician from testifying about information obtained in the course of his treatment by the physician. Thus, a legal affirmation of the ethical principle of **confidentiality**. See **privileged communication** following.

privileged communication: The laws of evidence in some jurisdictions provide that certain kinds of communications between persons who have a special confidential or fiduciary relationship will not be divulged. The psychotherapist-patient and doctor-patient relationship is in some states considered privileged communication. But the law is in a state of flux and there are many exceptions—e.g. a patient who sues, basing the suit in whole or in part on psychiatric considerations, may waive privilege.

right to treatment: The legal doctrine that a facility is legally obligated to provide adequate treatment for an individual when the facility has assumed the responsibility of providing treatment.

TABLE OF NEUROLOGIC DEFICITS

abulia: A reduction in impulse to action and thought coupled with indifference or lack of concern about the consequences of action.

acalculia: Loss of previously possessed facility with arithmetic calculation.

adiadochokinesia: Inability to perform rapid alternating movements of one or more of the extremities.

agnosia: Inability to recognize objects presented by way of one or more sensory modalities that cannot be explained by a defect in elementary sensation or a reduced level of consciousness or alertness.

   spatial agnosia: Inability to recognize spatial relations; disordered spatial orientation.

agraphia: Loss of a previously possessed facility for writing.

akathisia: A state of motor restlessness ranging from a feeling of inner disquiet to inability to sit still or lie quietly.

akinetic mutism: A state of apparent alertness with following eye movements but no speech or voluntary motor responses.

alexia: Loss of a previously possessed reading facility that cannot be explained by defective visual acuity.

anosognosia: The apparent unawareness of or failure of recognition of one's own functional defect; e.g. hemiplegia, hemianopia.

aphasia: Loss of a previously possessed facility of language comprehension or production which cannot be explained by sensory or motor defects or diffuse cerebral dysfunction.
   anomic or **amnestic aphasia:** Loss of the ability to name objects.
   Broca's aphasia: Loss of the ability to produce spoken and (usually) written language with comprehension retained.
   Wernicke's aphasia: Loss of the ability to comprehend language, coupled with production of inappropriate language.

apraxia: Loss of a previously possessed ability to perform skilled motor acts which cannot be explained by weakness, abnormal muscle tone or elementary incoordination.
   constructional apraxia: An acquired difficulty in drawing two-dimensional objects or forms, or in producing or copying three-dimensional arrangements of forms or shapes.

astereognosis: Inability to recognize familiar objects by touch that cannot be explained by a defect of elementary tactile sensation.

autotopagnosia: Inability to localize and name the parts of one's own body.
   finger agnosia: Autotopagnosia restricted to the fingers.

confabulation: Fabrication of stories in response to questions about situations or events that are not recalled.

dys: Prefix usually used to indicate that a function has never developed normally: thus **dyscalculia**, dysgraphia, **dyslexia**, dysphasia and dyspraxia. The prefix may also be used to indicate a perversion of normal function or an incomplete defect.

dysarthria: Difficulty in speech production due to incoordination of speech apparatus.

dysgeusia: Perversion of the sense of taste.

echolalia: Parrot-like repetition of overheard words or fragments of speech.

gegenhalten: "Active" resistance to passive movement of the extremities which does not appear to be under voluntary control.

perseveration: Tendency to emit the same verbal or motor response again and again to varied stimuli.

prosopagnosia: Inability to recognize familiar faces not explained by defective visual acuity or reduced consciousness or alertness.

sensory extinction: Failure to report sensory stimuli from one region if another region is stimulated simultaneously, even though when the region in question is stimulated by itself, the stimulus is correctly reported.

simultanagnosia: Inability to comprehend more than one element of a visual scene at the same time or to integrate the parts into a whole.

TABLE OF RESEARCH TERMS

attributable risk: The rate of the disorder in exposed individuals that can be attributed to the exposure, derived from subtracting the rate (usually incidence or mortality) of the disorder of the non-exposed population from the corresponding rate of the exposed population.

concordance: In genetic studies, the similarity in a twin pair with respect to the presence or absence of a disease or trait.

control group: The scores of this group are contrasted to the scores of the experimental group to counter the possibility that the experimental results might have occurred spontaneously over time, regardless of the experimental manipulation. Control groups are usually matched to experimental groups in terms of age, sex, and other characteristics that might be relevant.

correlation: The extent to which two variables co-relate or go together. This can be used to determine reliability of certain measures, and unexpected correlations can suggest areas for new research.

demand characteristics ("experimenter effects"): Refers to the experimenter who may and often does have strong feelings or expectations regarding the subjects of an experiment so that the subjects pick up the experimenter's cues and behave accordingly.

discordance: In genetic studies, dissimilarity in a twin pair with respect to the presence or absence of a disease or trait.

double-blind: A study in which one or more drugs and a **placebo** are compared in such way that neither the patient nor the persons directly or indirectly involved in the study know which preparation is being administered.

experimental study designs:

    case-control: An investigation in which groups of individuals are selected in terms of whether they do (cases) or do not (controls) have the disorder, the **etiology** of which is being studied.

    cohort: An important form of epidemiologic investigation to test hypotheses regarding the causation of disease. The distinguishing factors are: (1) the group or groups of persons to be studied (the cohorts) are defined in terms of characteristics evident prior to appearance of the disorder being investigated; (2) the study groups so defined are observed over a period of time to determine the frequency of the disorder among them.

    cross sectional: Study in which measurements of cause and effect are made at the same point in time, usually retrospectively.

    longitudinal: Study in which observations relate to two different points in time, even if both items of information are collected simultaneously. Most **cohort** and **case-control** studies are longitudinal.

prospective: Study based on data or events which occur subsequent in time relative to the initiation of the investigation. This type of study usually requires many years in order to develop a large enough study population.

retrospective: Study based on data or events which occurred prior in time relative to the investigation.

falsifiable hypothesis: A hypothesis that is stated in sufficiently precise a fashion that it is able to be tested by acceptable rules of logic and/or empirical evidence, and thereby found to be either confirmed or disconfirmed. An unfalsifiable hypothesis is one that is so general and/or ambiguous that all conceivable evidence can be "explained" by it.

heuristic: Imprecise in detail; serving to encourage further discovery. A quality that encourages students to discover for themselves.

incidence: The number of cases of disease which come into being during a specific period of time.

mean: The arithmetic average of a set of observations; the sum of scores divided by the number of scores.

median: The middle value in a set of values that have been arranged in order from highest to lowest; the number of values lying above it will equal the number of values lying below it.

mode: The most frequently occurring observation in a set of observations.

null hypothesis: The assumption that any observed difference between two samples of a statistical population is purely accidental and not due to a systematic cause; the assumption that observations have come from a population that is not different from a non-systematic population.

period prevalence: A measure that expresses the total number of cases of a disease known to have existed at some time during a specified period. It is the sum of **point prevalence** and **incidence.**

point prevalence: The frequency of the disease at a designated point in time.

practice effects: The improvement in task performance as a result of repeated trials or training in the task.

q-sort: A personality assessment technique in which the subject (or someone who observes him) indicates the degree to which a standardized set of descriptive statements actually describe the subject. The term reflects the "sorting" procedures occasionally used with this technique.

random sample: A group of subjects selected in such a way that each member of the group from which the sample is derived has an equal chance (probability) of being chosen for the sample.

relative risk: The ratio of the disorder (usually **incidence** or mortality) of those exposed to the rate of those not exposed.

75

reliability: Replicability; i.e. the extent to which the same test will yield the same results on repetition.

standard deviation (SD): A mathematical indication of the dispersion of scores clustered about the mean. In any distribution which approximates the normal curve in form, about 65% of the measures will lie within one SD of the mean, and about 95% will lie within two SDs of the mean.

type 1 error: Rejecting the **null hypothesis** when it is true; the minimum probability of making a type 1 error is usually called the "significance of the study."

type 2 error: Failing to reject a false **null hypothesis**.

validity: The degree to which a measure gives an indication of a particular quality or attribute that it claims to measure.

variable: Any characteristic in an experiment which may assume different values. A **dependent variable** is a characteristic whose value is linked to another condition of the experiment. An **independent variable** is a characteristic, ideally set up by the experimenter, which determines the outcome of the experiment.

zygosity: (1) **dizygotic:** fraternal twins, the product of two fertilized ova. They have the genetic relationship of any two **siblings**; (2) **monozygotic:** identical twins, the product of a single fertilized ovum.

TABLE OF SCHOOLS OF PSYCHIATRY

I. Reconstructive
  A. Psychoanalysis—Sigmund **Freud**
  B. Neo-Freudian, modifications of psychoanalysis
    1. Active analytic techniques—Sandor Ferenczi, Wilhelm Stekel, the Chicago school (especially Franz Alexander and Thomas French)
    2. Analytic play therapy—Anna **Freud**, Melanie **Klein**
    3. Analytical psychology—Carl **Jung**
    4. Character analysis, orgone therapy—Wilhelm **Reich**
    5. Cognitive—Jean **Piaget**
    6. Developmental—Erik **Erikson**
    7. Ego psychology—Paul Federn, Edoardo Weiss, Heinz Hartmann, Ernst Kris, Rudolph Loewenstein
    8. Existential analysis—Ludwig Binswanger
    9. Holistic analysis—Karen **Horney**
    10. Individual psychology—Alfred **Adler**
    11. Transactional analysis—Eric Berne
    12. Washington cultural school—Harry Stack **Sullivan**, Erich Fromm, Clara Thompson
    13. Will therapy—Otto **Rank**
  C. Group Approaches
    1. Orthodox psychoanalytic—S. R. Slavson
    2. Psychodrama—Jacob L. Moreno
    3. Psychonalysis in groups—Alexander Wolf
    4. Valence systems—Walter Bion

II. Reeducative and Supportive, Individual and Group
    1. Client-centered (non-directive)—Carl Rogers
    2. Conditioning, behavior therapy, behavior modification
      a. aversion therapy—N. V. Kantorovich
      b. behaviorism—John B. **Watson**
      c. classical conditioning—Ivan **Pavlov**
      d. operant conditioning—Burrhus F. **Skinner**
      e. sexual counseling—William Masters, Virginia Johnson
      f. systematic desensitization—Joseph Wolpe
    3. Family therapy—Nathan Ackerman
    4. Gestalt—Wolfgang Kohler, Kurt Lewin, Fritz Perls
    5. Logotherapy—Victor Frankl
    6. Psychobiology (distributive analysis and synthesis)—Adolf **Meyer**
    7. Zen (satori)—Alan Watts

TABLE OF PSYCHOLOGICAL TESTS

Test	Type	Assesses	Age of Patient	Output	Administration
Bayley Scales of Infant Development	Infant development	Cognitive functioning & motor development	1–30 months	Performance on subtests measuring cognitive & motor development	Individual
Bender Visual-Motor Gestalt Test	Projective visual-motor development	Personality conflicts Ego function and structure Organic brain damage	5–Adult	Patient's reproduction of geometric figures	Individual
Benton Visual Retention Test	Objective performance	Organic brain damage	Adult	Patient's reproduction of geometric figures from memory	Individual
Cattell Infant Intelligence Scale	Infant development	General motor & cognitive development	1–18 months	Performance on developmental tasks	Individual

Test	Type	Measures	Age	Description	Administration
Draw-A-Person **Draw-A-Family** **House-Tree-Person**	Projective	Personality conflicts Self-image (DAP) Family perception (DAF) Ego functions Intellectual functioning (DAP) Visual-motor coordination	2–Adult	Patient's drawings on a blank sheet of paper	Individual
Frostig (Marianne) Developmental Test of Visual Perception	Visual perception	Eye-motor coordination Figure ground perception Constancy of shape Position in space Spatial relationships	4–8 years	Performance on paper and pencil test measuring five aspects of visual perception	Individual or Group
Gesell Developmental Schedules	Preschool development	Cognitive, motor, language and social development	1–60 months	Performance on developmental tasks	Individual

Test	Type	Assesses	Age of Patient	Output	Administration
Illinois Test of Psycholinguistic Ability (ITPA)	Language ability	Auditory-vocal, visual motor channels of language receptive, organizational, & expressive components	2–10 years	Performance on 12 sub-tests measuring various dimensions of language functioning	Individual
Minnesota Multiphasic Personality Inventory (MMPI)	Paper and pencil personality inventory	Personality structure Diagnostic classification	Adolescent– Adult	Personality profile reflecting nine dimensions of personality Diagnosis based upon actuarial prediction	Group

Test	Type	Measures	Age	Description	Administration
Otis Quick Scoring Mental Abilities Tests	Intelligence	Intellectual functioning	5–Adult	Performance on verbal and nonverbal dimensions of intellectual functioning	Group
Rorschach	Projective	Personality conflicts Ego function and structure Defensive structure Thought processes Affective integration	3–Adult	Patient's associations to inkblots	Individual
Stanford-Binet	Intelligence	Intellectual functioning	2–Adult	Performance on problem solving and developmental tasks	Individual

Test	Type	Assesses	Age of Patient	Output	Administration
Thematic Apperception Test (TAT) **Michigan Picture Stories** **Tasks of Emotional Develop. (TED)** **Child's Apperception Test (CAT)**	Projective	Personality conflicts Defensive structure	Adult—TAT Adolescent—Mich. Picture Stories Child & adolescent—TED Child—CAT	Patient makes up stories after viewing stimulus pictures	Individual
Vineland Social Maturity Scale	Social maturity	Capacity for independent functioning	0–25+ years	Performance on developmental tasks measuring various dimensions of social functioning	Interview parent or guardian of patient, occasionally self-report

Wechsler Adult Intelligence Scale (WAIS)	Intelligence	Intellectual functioning Thought processes Ego functioning	16–Adult	Performance on 10 sub-tests measuring various dimensions of intellectual functioning	Individual
Wechsler Intelligence Scale for Children (WISC)	Intelligence	Intellectual functioning Thought processes Ego functioning	5–15	See above	Individual
Wechsler Preschool and Primary Scale of Intelligence (WPPSI)	Intelligence	Intellectual functioning Thought processes Ego functioning	4–6½ years	See above	Individual

TABLE OF SLEEP DISORDERS*

PRIMARY SLEEP DISORDERS
(disordered sleep is the only sign and symptom of abnormality)

Disorder	Clinical Findings	EEG Findings	Treatment
cataplexy	Sudden decrease or loss of muscle tone, often generalized. May be precipitated by laughter, anger, or surprise. Eye muscles are not paralyzed. If person supine, sleep may follow.	Ensuing sleep lapses directly into REM state.	Imipramine.
hypersomnia, chronic	Excessive sleep at night or during day. None of the findings associated with **narcolepsy**. Post sleep confusion. Increased cardiac and respiratory rates. **Depression** may be present. Can occur with **central nervous system** damage.	Normal sleep EEG.	Treatment for any other disorder present.
insomnia	Inability to fall asleep and difficulty staying asleep including early morning awakening. As a primary sleep disorder, it occurs in the absence of physical or psychological illness.	Longer time before sleep onset. Short sleeping time. Greater physiologic arousal during sleep. Increased REM sleep.	Hypnotic drugs and supportive treatment.
Kleine-Levin syndrome	Periodic episodes (about every 6 months) of hypersomnia. First appears in **adolescence**, usually in boys and is accompanied by **bulimia**.	Various findings. Some show absence of sleep spindles.	Eventual spontaneous disappearance of syndrome.

narcolepsy	Uncontrollable, recurrent, brief episodes of sleep associated with **cataplexy**, sleep paralysis (inability to move occurring at waking) and **hypnagogic hallucinations** (occurs as the person falls asleep). Disturbed nocturnal sleep is also present.	REM episode begins with sleep onset.	Amphetamines or methylphenidate.
nightmares (dream anxiety attacks)	Mild anxiety and **autonomic** reactions. Good recall of dream. Contrast with **night terrors.**	Occurs during REM sleep.	Reassurance. Psychotherapy if severe.
night terrors (pavor nocturnus)	Extreme panic, verbalizations, **autonomic** activity, confusion, poor recall for event. **Psychopathology** rare in children, common in adults with the disorder. Contrast with **nightmares.**	Occurs during stage 4 sleep.	Children—reassure parents. Adults—possible use of medication to suppress stage 4 sleep.
Pickwickian syndrome	Obesity, respiratory irregularities and **hypersomnia**. Sleep associated with periods of apnea (no breathing). Sleep is discontinuous.	EEG signs of arousal at end of each apneic period. Little or no slow wave of REM sleep.	

* See definition of **sleep** in alphabetical listing.

SECONDARY SLEEP DISORDERS
(clinical problems accompanied by specific or nonspecific sleep disturbances.)

alcoholic psychoses*	Variable.	Slow wave and REM sleep suppressed during acute alcoholic state, following an initial increase. Withdrawal results in rebound of slow wave and REM sleep.
anorexia nervosa*	Decreased total sleep time.	Decreased stages 3, 4 and REM sleep. Increased time before onset of stage 1, 3 and REM sleep.
depression*	Less sleep time, more awakenings.	Less slow wave sleep. REM state findings vary. Decreased time before REM sleep and decreased intervals between REM periods.
hyperthyroidism	Insomnia.	Stages 3 and 4 increased.
hypothyroidism	Increased somnolence.	Stages 3 and 4 decreased.
schizophrenia*	Variable.	Much less slow wave sleep. REM debt related to symptoms.

* See definition of these terms in alphabetical listing.

PARASOMNIAS
(waking type behavior occurring during sleep.)

bruxism (teeth grinding)	Loud noises and eventual damage to teeth and supporting structures.	Occurs during stage 2 sleep. Sleep stages not disturbed.	Removal of dental problems. Use of dental prosthesis to discourage biting.
enuresis*	In boys and men predominantly. May be familial. Excessive bladder contractions during sleep and higher heart rates.	Can occur during all sleep stages but often associated with stage 4. Not related to dreaming.	Parental guidance, training, imipramine.
sleep talking	Very common by itself or as part of other sleep disorders, psychological or organic disorders.	Mainly during NREM sleep. Occasionally during REM sleep.	
sleep walking (somnabulism)	Mainly in boys and men. Often accompanied by **night terrors** and **enuresis**. Forced awakening accompanied by confusion.	Occurs during stage 4 sleep.	Children often outgrow. Adults often have psychiatric disturbance.

*See definition of these terms in alphabetical listing.

SLEEP EXACERBATED DISORDERS

Disorder	Clinical and EEG Findings	Treatment
bronchial asthma	In adults, attacks unrelated to sleep stage. In children, attacks generally do not occur during first part of night when stage 4 sleep predominates. Adults and children have decreased amounts of stage 4 sleep and less total sleep time.	
coronary artery disease	REM sleep associated with changes in heart rate, respiration and blood pressure. Nocturnal angina associated with REM sleep.	Avoid drugs which result in REM rebound.
duodenal ulcer	Greatly increased gastric acid secretion at night compared to normal people. Peak acid secretion during REM sleep.	Avoid drugs which result in REM rebound.

inhibition: In psychiatry, an *unconscious defense* against forbidden instinctual *drives;* it may interfere with or restrict specific activities or general patterns of behavior.

insane: Obsolete term for *mental disorder.* Still used, however, in strictly legal contexts such as *insanity defense.* See *Table of Legal Terms,* p. 70.

insanity: A vague, legal term for *psychosis,* now obsolete.

insanity defense: See *Table of Legal Terms,* p. 70.

insight: Self-understanding. The extent of the individual's understanding of the origin, nature, and mechanisms of his attitudes and behavior. More superficially, recognition by a patient that he is ill.

insomnia: See *sleep, Table of Sleep Disorders,* p. 84.

instinct: An inborn *drive.* The primary human instincts include self-preservation and sexuality and—for some proponents—*aggression,* the *ego instincts,* and "herd" or "social" instincts, *Freud* also postulated a *death instinct.*

instrumental conditioning: See *conditioning* under *behavior therapy.*

insulin coma treatment: See *shock treatment.*

integration: The useful organization and incorporation of both new and old data, experience, and emotional capacities into the *personality.* Also refers to the organization and amalgamation of functions at various levels of *psychosexual development.*

intellectualization: The utilization of reasoning as a *defense* against confrontation with *unconscious conflicts* and their stressful *emotions.*

intelligence: Capacity to learn and to utilize appropriately what one has learned. May be affected by *emotions.*

intelligence quotient (IQ): A numerical rating determined through psychological testing that indicates the approximate relationship of a person's mental age (MA) to his chronological age (CA). Expressed mathematically as $IQ = \dfrac{MA}{CA} \times 100$. See *Table of Psychological Tests,* p. 78.

International Classification of Diseases (ICD): The official list of disease categories issued by the World Health Organization. Subscribed to by all WHO member nations, who may assign their own terms to each ICD category. ICDA (*International Classification of Diseases, Adapted for Use in the United States*), prepared by the U.S. Public Health Service, represents the official list of diagnostic terms to be used for each ICD category in this country. *DSM-II* is based upon the eighth revision of the International Classification of Diseases (ICD-8) prepared in 1966.

interpretation: The process by which the therapist communicates to the patient understanding of a particular aspect of his problems or behavior.

intrapsychic: That which takes place within the *psyche* or mind.

intrapsychic conflict: See under *conflict*.

introjection: A *defense mechanism*, operating *unconsciously*, whereby loved or hated external objects are taken within oneself symbolically. The converse of *projection*. May serve as a defense against *conscious* recognition of intolerable hostile impulses. For example, in severe *depression*, the individual may unconsciously direct unacceptable hatred or *aggression* toward himself, i.e. toward the introjected object within himself. Related to the more primitive mechanism of *incorporation*.

introversion: Preoccupation with oneself and accompanying reduction of interest in the outside world; the reverse of *extraversion*.

involutional melancholia (involutional psychosis): See under *depression*.

involutional paranoid state (involutional paraphrenia): See under *paranoid states*.

IQ: See *intelligence quotient*.

irresistible impulse test: See *Table of Legal Terms*, p. 70.

isolation: A *defense mechanism*, operating *unconsciously*, in which an unacceptable impulse, idea, or act is separated from its original memory source, thereby removing the emotional charge associated with the original memory.

ITPA: Illinois Test of Psycholinguistic Ability. See *Table of Psychological Tests,* p. 78.

J

Jacksonian epilepsy: See *epilepsy.*

Janet, Pierre (1859–1947): French *psychiatrist.* Described *psychasthenia,* which is sometimes referred to as Janet's disease. Also first to use term *la belle indifference.*

Joint Commission on Accreditation of Hospitals: The agency which surveys and accredits hospitals of all kinds as fulfilling its standards. See also *accreditation.*

Joint Commission on Mental Health of Children: A multi-disciplinary agency authorized by the U. S. Congress in 1965 (Public Law 89–97) and established in 1966 to study and report on the nation's "resources, methods, and practices for diagnosing or preventing emotional illness in children and of treating, caring for, and rehabilitating children with emotional illness." Its final report, titled *Crisis in Child Mental Health: Challenge for the 1970s* was published in 1969.

Joint Commission on Mental Illness and Health: A multi-disciplinary agency, incorporated in 1956, and representing thirty-six national agencies in the *mental health* and welfare fields. It conducted a five-year study of the mental health needs of the nation between 1956 and 1961 as authorized by the U.S. Congress in the Mental Health Study Act of 1955. The final report of the Joint Commission, *Action for Mental Health,* led ultimately to legislation by the Congress in 1964 authorizing and appropriating funds to facilitate the development of *community mental health centers* for the mentally ill and mentally retarded in the several states.

Jones, Ernest (1879–1958): English *psychoanalyst* and early pupil of *Freud* and his principal biographer. He pioneered in introducing *psychoanalysis* to the English-speaking world.

Journal of Hospital and Community Psychiatry: The official monthly journal of the Hospital and Community Psychiatry Service of the *American Psychiatric Association*.

Jung, Carl Gustav (1875–1961): Swiss *psychoanalyst*. Founder of the school of *analytic psychology*.

K

kinesics (kinesiology): The study of body movement as a part of the process of communication; sociological analysis of interactional activity. Of all the continuous muscular shifts that are characteristic of human beings, some groupings of movements are utilized by the social system for communication purposes. *Body language* is a learned form of communication that is patterned by the culture and tends to be highly specific for particular social groups within the context in which it appears. Kinesics, the study of the meaning of body posture, movement and facial expression, and *linguistics*, the study of words and language, are directed toward the isolation and analysis of infracommunication systems as a way to reduce the data of interactional behavior to objective, significant, measurable and manipulatable units.

Kirkbride, Thomas S. (1809–1883): American *psychiatrist*: one of the founders of the *American Psychiatric Association*. Noted for his pioneer contributions to mental hospital design.

Klein, Melanie (1882–1960): British child *psychoanalyst* who pioneered the *psychoanalysis* of children. Noted for her work on early childhood development, particularly infantile aggression and the origins of the *superego* in early infancy. See *Table of Schools of Psychiatry*, p. 77.

Kleine-Levin syndrome: See *Table of Sleep Disorders*, p. 84.

kleptomania: See *-mania*.

Klinefelters syndrome: *Chromosomal* defect in which there is an extra sex x-chromosome. Manifestations of this syndrome may include testicular atrophy and physical feminization in a male.

Klüver-Bucy syndrome: Due to bilateral temporal lobe ablation. Characterized by loss of recognition of people, loss of *fear*, rage reactions, hypersexuality, excessive oral behavior, memory defect, and overreactivity to visual stimuli.

koro: See *culture specific syndromes*.

Korsakoff's psychosis: See *Wernicke-Korsakoff syndrome*.

Kraepelin, Emil (1885–1926): German *psychiatrist* who developed an extensive systematic classification of mental diseases. One of the first workers to delineate the concept of *dementia praecox* or *schizophrenia*. See also *descriptive psychiatry*.

L

la belle indifference: Literally, "beautiful indifference." Seen in certain patients with *hysterical neurosis, conversion type* (see *neurosis*), who show an inappropriate lack of concern about their disabilities.

labile: Pertaining to rapidly shifting emotions; unstable.

lapsus linguae: A slip of the tongue due to *unconscious* factors.

latah: See *culture specific syndromes*.

latency period: See *psychosexual development*.

latent content: The hidden (*unconscious*) meaning of thoughts or actions, especially in dreams or fantasies. In dreams it is expressed in distorted, disguised, condensed, and symbolic form, which is known as the *manifest content*.

latent homosexuality: A condition characterized by *unconscious* homosexual desires. See *homosexuality*.

learned autonomic control: See *biofeedback*.

learning disability: A syndrome affecting school age children of normal or above normal intelligence characterized by specific difficulties in learning to read (*dyslexia*), write (dysgraphia), and calculate (dyscalculia). The disorder appears related to slow developmental progression of perceptual motor skills. See also *minimal brain dysfunction*.

lesbian: *Homosexual* woman.

lesbianism: Homosexual activity between women. See also *homosexuality, sexual orientation disturbance.*

libido: The psychic *drive* or energy usually associated with the sexual *instinct.* (Sexual is used here in the broad sense to include pleasure and love-object seeking.)

linguistics: See *kinesics (kinesiology), body language.*

lithium carbonate: The particular lithium salt usually used in the treatment of acute *manic* states and in the prevention of future episodes in individuals with recurrent *affective disorders* which may be either unipolar (*depression* or *mania* only) or bipolar (both mania and depression occasionally occurring). The utility of this drug in the treatment of mania was originally discovered by Cade, an Australian. The dose of lithium carbonate used is determined by monitoring the level in the patient's serum. Signs of toxicity may include nausea, vomiting, diarrhea, tremor, dizziness, *dysarthria,* drowsiness and ataxia. See also *Table of Drugs Used in Psychiatry,* p. 68.

logorrhea: Uncontrollable, excessive talking.

loosening (of associations): A thinking disorder, or disturbance in associations, in which thinking becomes over-generalized, diffuse and vague, progressing unevenly towards a goal and generally failing as an adequate vehicle of communication with others. The associations may be irrelevant (not appropriately related to the theme under discussion), or circumstantial (bogged down in a morass of trivial details that impede rather than enhance the understanding of the listener) or tangential (about a topic clearly separate and removed from the theme). Loosening is a characteristic of many *schizophrenic* patients.

LP: See *lumbar puncture.*

LSD (lysergic acid diethylamide): A potent drug that produces psychotic symptoms and behavior. The symptoms may include *hallucinations, illusions, delusions,* and time-space distortions.

lumbar puncture: The insertion of a long needle between the lumbar vertebrae into the meningeal sac around the base of the spinal cord to obtain cerebrospinal fluid for neurological diagnostic purposes.

95

M

magical thinking: A person's conviction that thinking equates with doing. Occurs in dreams, in children and primitive peoples, and in patients under a variety of conditions. Characterized by lack of realistic relationship between cause and effect.

major affective disorders: A group of *psychoses* characterized by severe disorders of mood—either extreme *depression* or elation or both—that do not seem to be attributable entirely to precipitating life experiences. Includes *involutional melancholia* and the varieties of *manic-depressive psychosis*.

major epilepsy (grand mal): See under *epilepsy*.

maladjustment: See *adaptation*.

maleness: Anatomic and physiologic features which relate to the male's procreative capacity. See also *masculine*.

malingering: Deliberate simulation or exaggeration of an illness or disability that, in fact, is nonexistent or minor, in order to avoid an unpleasant situation or to obtain some type of personal gain. See also *compensation neurosis* and *secondary gain*.

-mania: Formerly used as a nonspecific term for any kind of "madness." Currently used as a suffix with any number of Greek roots to indicate a morbid preoccupation with some kind of idea or activity, and/or a *compulsive* need to behave in some deviant way. *Phobia* as a suffix is used in a similar way. For example:

dipsomania: Compulsion to drink alcoholic beverages.

96

egomania: Pathological preoccupation with self.

erotomania: Pathological preoccupation with erotic fantasies or activities.

kleptomania: Compulsion to steal.

megalomania: Pathological preoccupation with *delusions* of power or wealth.

monomania: Pathological preoccupation with one subject.

necromania: Pathological preoccupation with dead bodies.

nymphomania: Abnormal and excessive need or desire in the woman for sexual intercourse. See also *erotomania, satyriasis*.

pyromania: Morbid compulsion to set fires.

trichotillomania: Compulsion to pull out one's hair.

mania: A mood disorder characterized by excessive elation, hyperactivity, agitation, and accelerated thinking and speaking, sometimes manifested as *flight of ideas*. Mania is seen most frequently as one of the two major forms of *manic-depressive psychosis*.

maniac: Imprecise, sensational, and misleading lay term for an emotionally disturbed person. Usually implies violent behavior. Is not specifically referable to any psychiatric diagnostic category.

manic-depressive psychosis: A *major affective disorder* characterized by severe mood swings and a tendency to remission and recurrence. It is divided into the following three sub-groups:

circular type: An illness distinguished by at least one depressive episode and a manic episode. See *bipolar psychosis*.

depressed type: A depressive illness consisting exclusively of depressive episodes characterized by severely depressed mood and by mental and motor retardation that may progress to stupor. Uneasiness, apprehension, perplexity, and agitation may also be present. See *unipolar depression*.

manic type: An illness consisting of manic episodes characterized by excessive elation, irritability, talkativeness, flight of ideas, and accelerated speech and motor activity.
See also *depression*.

manifest content: The remembered content of a dream or fantasy, as contrasted with *latent content*, which it conceals and distorts.

97

mantra: See *biofeedback.*

MAO inhibitor (MAOI): *Monoamine oxidase inhibitor.*

marathon group: Extremely long group meeting (8-72 hours) the goal of which is to develop intimate interaction and openness that prolonged contact might facilitate. Sometimes used in conjunction with *group psychotherapy.*

marital counseling: A treatment modality whose goal is to ameliorate problems of married couples. Various psychodynamic, sexual, ethical, and economic aspects of marriage are considered. Husband and wife are usually seen individually and conjointly. A broader term is *couples therapy* which encompasses unmarried couples.

masculine: An adjective to describe a set of sex specific social role behaviors that are unrelated to procreative biologic function. See also *gender identity, gender role* and *maleness.*

masculine protest: Term coined by Alfred *Adler* to describe a striving to escape *identification* with the feminine role. Applies primarily to women but may also be noted in men.

masochism: Pleasure derived from physical or psychological pain inflicted either by one's self or by others. When it is *consciously* sought as a part of the sexual act or as a prerequisite to sexual gratification, it is classifiable as a *sexual deviation.* It is the converse of *sadism,* and the two tend to coexist in the same individual.

masturbation: Genital manipulation for the purpose of sexual stimulation. A normal activity from infancy through adulthood.

maximum security unit: A building or ward in a mental hospital or other institutional setting especially designed to prevent the escape of mental patients who have committed crimes or whose symptoms are a physical threat to the safety of others. See also *criminally insane.*

mean: See *Table of Research Terms,* p. 74.

median: See *Table of Research Terms,* p. 74.

medical psychotherapy: See *psychotherapy, medical.*

Medicare: The hospital insurance system and the supplementary medical insurance for the aged created by the 1965 amendments to the Social Security Act. The insurance provides the same hospital benefits in general hospitals for psychiatric conditions as for other conditions but limits benefits in psychiatric hospitals to 190 days during a lifetime.

megalomania: See *-mania.*

megavitamin therapy: See *orthomolecular treatment.*

melancholia: See *involutional melancholia.*

memory disturbances: See *organic brain syndrome.*

menarche: The onset of menstruation.

mens rea: See *Table of Legal Terms,* p. 70.

mental deficiency: See *mental retardation.*

mental disease: See *mental disorder.*

mental disorder: Any psychiatric illness or disease included in the World Health Organization's *International Classification of Diseases,* or in the American Psychiatric Association's *Diagnostic and Statistical Manual of Mental Disorders,* Second Edition (1968). Many of these disorders are defined in this glossary.

mental health: A state of being, relative rather than absolute, in which a person has effected a reasonably satisfactory integration of his *instinctual drives.* His integration is acceptable to himself and to his social milieu as reflected in his interpersonal relationships, his level of satisfaction in living, his actual achievement, his flexibility, and the level of maturity he has attained.

mental hygiene: Measures employed to reduce the *incidence* of mental disorders through prevention and early treatment and to promote *mental health.*

mental illness: Same as *mental disorder.*

mental mechanism: A generic term for a variety of psychic processes that are functions of the *ego* and largely *unconscious.* Includes *perception,* memory, thinking, and *defense mechanisms.*

99

mental retardation: Significantly below average intellectual functioning which may be present at birth or become evident later in the developmental period and is always characterized by impaired adaptation in one or all of the areas of learning, social adjustment and maturation. Emotional disturbance is often present. The term is descriptive of the current status of the individual relative to the group in which he functions. Causes of mental retardation include: infections occurring during early pregnancy such as rubella (German measles); *encephalitis*; injury at or following birth; metabolic disorders such as *phenylketonuria* or nutritional disorders including malnutrition; chromosomal abnormalities such as *Down's syndrome*; social and psychological factors such as emotional deprivation and decreased environmental stimulation in infancy and childhood.

The degree of retardation is measured in terms of IQ (*intelligence quotient*): borderline (70-85), mild (50-70), moderate (35-50), severe (20-35), and profound (under 20). If the IQ is above 50, the person is usually educable which means that academic achievement at the fourth to fifth grade level can be attained and the person's adjustment may include self-support. The moderately retarded are trainable which means they can achieve self-care, social adjustment at home and economic usefulness in a closely supervised environment. The severely and profoundly retarded usually require institutional care.

mental status: The level and style of functioning of the *psyche*, used in its broadest sense to include intellectual functioning as well as the emotional, attitudinal, psychological and personality aspects of the subject; in clinical psychiatry, the term is commonly used to refer to the results of the examination of the patient's mental state. Such an examination ordinarily aims to achieve one or more of the following: (1) evaluation and assessment of any psychiatric condition present including provisional diagnosis and prognosis, determination of degree of impairment, suitability for treatment, and indications for particular types of therapeutic intervention; (2) formulation of the personality structure of the subject, which may suggest the historical and developmental antecedents of whatever psychiatric condition exists; (3) estimate of the ability and willingness of the subject to participate appropriately in the treatment regimen considered desirable for him. The

100

mental status is reported in a series of narrative statements describing such things as: *affect*, speech, thought content, perception and cognitive functions, including *orientation*. The mental status is a part of the general examination of all patients, although it may be markedly abbreviated in the absence of *psychopathology*.

mental status examination: The process of estimating psychological and behavioral function by observing the patient, eliciting the patient's subjective description of himself and formally questioning the patient.

mescaline: An alkaloid orginally derived from the peyote cactus, resembling *amphetamine* and adrenalin chemically; used to induce altered perceptions. Used by Indians of the Southwest in religious rites.

mesmerism: Early term for *hypnosis*. Named after Anton Mesmer (1733–1815).

mesomorphic: See *constitutional types*.

metapsychiatry: The interface between *psychiatry* and such psychic phenomena as *parapsychology*, mysticism, transcendental meditation, *biofeedback*, and all other suprasensory, suprarational, esoteric manifestations of consciousness that are in any way relevant to the theory and practice of psychiatry.

metapsychology: The branch of theoretical or speculative *psychology* that deals with the significance of mental processes; the nature of the mind-body interrelationship; the origin, purpose, and structure of the mind; and similar hypotheses that are beyond the realm of empirical verification.

Methadone: A synthetic narcotic. It may be used as a substitute for heroin, producing a less socially disabling *addiction*, or it may be used to aid in the withdrawal from heroin. See also *narcotic blockade*.

Metrazol shock treatment: See *shock treatment*.

Meyer, Adolf (1866–1950): American *psychiatrist*, longtime professor of psychiatry at Johns Hopkins University, who formulated and

101

introduced the concept of *psychobiology*. See *Table of Schools of Psychiatry*, p. 77.

Michigan Picture Stories: See *Table of Psychological Tests*, p. 78.

migraine: A syndrome characterized by recurrent, severe, and usually one-sided headaches, often associated with nausea, vomiting, and visual disturbances.

milieu therapy: Socioenvironmental therapy in which the attitudes and behavior of the staff of a treatment service and the activities prescribed for the patient are determined by what the patient's emotional and interpersonal needs are presumed to be. This therapy is an essential part of all inpatient treatment. A patient whose basic problem is perceived as fear of authority figures, for example, might be placed in activities where freedom of expression, independence of action and competitiveness are fostered, and surrounded by warm, friendly and protecting personnel who can accept aggression and hostility without rancor or punitive retaliation.

minimal brain dysfunction: A disturbance of children and *adolescents* of normal or above normal intelligence without signs of major neurologic or psychiatric disturbance characterized by decreased attention span, distractability, increased activity, impulsivity, emotional *lability*, poor motor integration, disturbances in perception and disorders of language development. See *learning disability*.

Minnesota Multiphasic Personality Inventory (MMPI): See *Table of Psychological Tests*, p. 78.

minor epilepsy (petit mal): See under *epilepsy*.

Mitchell, S. Weir (1830–1914): American *neurologist*, who described *causalgia* and developed a once popular "rest cure" for emotional disorders.

MMPI (Minnesota Multiphasic Personality Inventory): See *Table of Psychological Tests*, p. 78.

M'Naghten Rule: See *Table of Legal Terms*, p. 70.

102

mode: See *Table of Research Terms,* p. 74.

mongolism: See *Down's syndrome.*

monoamine oxidase inhibitor (MAOI): A group of antidepressant drugs that inhibit certain brain enzymes and raise the level of *serotonin.* See *Table of Drugs Used in Psychiatry,* p. 68.

monomania: See *-mania.*

moral treatment: A philosophy and technique of treating mental patients that prevailed in the first half of the nineteenth century. It emphasized removal of restraints, humane and kindly care, attention to religion, and performance of useful tasks in the hospital.

moron: Obsolete term for an individual with borderline or mild *mental retardation.*

multiple personality: A term used by Morton *Prince* for a rare type of dissociative reaction in which the individual adopts two or more different personalities. See *hysterical neurosis, dissociative type,* under *neurosis.*

Münchausen syndrome (pathomimicry): A rare, difficult to treat disorder. Sufferers habitually attempt to hospitalize themselves with self-defined or self-induced pathology yearning for a surgical remedy. No definitive *etiology* has been established.

mutation: A change in hereditary constitution that causes genetically transmissible permanent differences between the characteristics of an individual and those of his parents; may occur spontaneously or may be induced by such agents as high-energy radiation. See also *genes.*

mutism: Refusal to speak for *conscious* or *unconscious* reasons. Often seen in *psychosis.*

mysophobia: See *phobia.*

N

narcissism (narcism): From Narcissus, figure in Greek mythology who fell in love with his own reflected image. Self-love, as opposed to object-love (love of another person). In psychoanalytic theory, cathexis (investment) of the psychic representation of the self with libido (sexual interest and energy). Some degree of narcissism is considered healthy and normal, but an excess interferes with relations with others. To be distinguished from egotism, which carries the connotation of self-centeredness, selfishness, and conceit. Egotism is but one expression of narcissism. See also *cathexis*, and *libido*.

narcoanalysis: See *narcosynthesis*.

narcolepsy: See *sleep, Table of Sleep Disorders*, p. 84.

narcosis: *Stupor*, of varying depth, induced by certain drugs.

narcosynthesis: Psychotherapeutic treatment under partial *anesthesia*, e.g. as induced by barbiturates. Originally used to treat acute mental disorders occurring in a military combat setting.

narcotic: Any opiate derivative drug, natural or synthetic, that relieves pain or alters mood. May cause *addiction*. See also *drug dependency, hypnotic, sedative*.

narcotic blockade: Total or partial inhibition of the *euphoria* produced by *narcotic* drugs through the use of other drugs, such as *Methadone*.

National Association for Mental Health: Leading voluntary citizens' organization in the mental health field. Founded in 1909 by Clifford W. *Beers* as the National Committee for Mental Hygiene.

National Institute of Alcohol Abuse and Alcoholism: See *Alcohol, Drug Abuse,* and *Mental Health Administration (ADAMHA).*

National Institute of Drug Abuse: See *Alcohol, Drug Abuse,* and *Mental Health Administration (ADAMHA).*

National Institute of Mental Health: See *Alcohol, Drug Abuse,* and *Mental Health Administration (ADAMHA).*

necromania: See *-mania.*

negativism: Opposition and resistance to suggestions or advice. Seen normally in late infancy. A common symptom in catatonic *schizophrenia.*

neologism: A new word or condensed combination of several words coined by a person to express a highly complex idea often related to his conflicts; not readily understood by others; seen in *schizophrenia* and *organic brain disorders.*

neoplasm: A new growth or tumor. Neoplasms that affect behavior are primarily, but not exclusively, found within the cranial cavity. Such neoplasms may cause mental and behavioral disturbances in addition to neurological signs and symptoms. See *organic brain syndromes.*

nervous breakdown: A nonmedical, nonspecific euphemism for a *mental disorder.*

neurasthenic neurosis (neurasthenia): See under *neurosis.*

neurologist: A physician with postgraduate training and experience in the field of organic diseases of the nervous system whose professional work focuses primarily on this area. Neurologists also receive training in *psychiatry.*

neurology: The branch of medical science devoted to the study, diagnosis, and treatment of organic diseases of the nervous system.

neuropsychiatry: Combination of the specialties of *neurology* and *psychiatry.*

neuroleptic: A psychotropic drug. See *Table of Drugs Used in Psychiatry*, p. 68.

neurosis (psychoneurosis): An emotional maladaptation arising from an unresolved *unconscious conflict*. The *anxiety* is either felt directly or modified by various psychological mechanisms to produce other, subjectively distressing symptoms. The neuroses are usually considered less severe than the *psychoses* (although not always less disabling) because they manifest neither gross personality disorganization nor gross distortion or misinterpretation of external reality. The neuroses are classified according to the predominating symptoms. The common neuroses are:

    anxiety neurosis: A neurosis characterized by anxious over-concern occasionally progressing to *panic*; frequently associated with somatic symptoms.

    depersonalization neurosis: A neurosis characterized by feelings of unreality and of estrangement from the self, body, or surroundings. Different from the process of *depersonalization*, which may be a manifestation of normal *anxiety* or of another mental disorder.

    depressive neurosis: A neurosis manifested by an excessive reaction of *depression* due to an internal conflict or to an identifiable event, such as a loss of a loved person or a cherished possession.

    hypochondriacal neurosis: A neurosis characterized by preoccupation with the body and with fear of presumed diseases of various organs. Although the fears are not *delusional* in quality, they persist despite reassurance.

    hysterical neurosis: A neurosis characterized by a sudden *psychogenic* loss or disorder of function in response to an emotional stress. This disorder is divided into two subtypes:

        conversion type: An hysterical neurosis manifested by disorders of the special senses or the voluntary nervous system, such as blindness, deafness, *anesthesia*, *paresthesia*, pain, paralysis, and impaired muscular coordination. A patient with this disorder may show *la belle indifference* about his symptoms, which may actually provide *secondary gains* by winning

106

him sympathy or relieving him of unpleasant responsibilities. See also *conversion*.

dissociative type: An hysterical neurosis manifested by alterations in the patient's state of consciousness or in his *identity*, producing such symptoms as *amnesia, somnambulism, fugue,* or *multiple personality*. See also *dissociation*.

neurasthenic neurosis (neurasthenia): A neurosis characterized by complaints of chronic weakness, easy fatigability, and exhaustion.

obsessive compulsive neurosis: A neurosis characterized by the persistent intrusion of unwanted thoughts, urges, or actions that the individual is unable to stop. The thoughts may consist of single words or ideas, ruminations, or trains of thought that the individual often views as nonsensical. The actions may vary from simple movements to complex rituals, such as repeated handwashing. See also *compulsion*.

phobic neurosis: A neurosis characterized by intense *fear* of an object or situation that the individual *consciously* recognizes as harmless. His apprehension may be experienced as faintness, fatigue, palpations, perspiration, nausea, tremor, and even *panic*. See also *phobia*.

night hospital: See *partial hospitalization*.

nightmares (dream anxiety attacks): See *Table of Sleep Disorders,* p. 84.

night terrors (pavor nocturnus): See *Table of Sleep Disorders,* p. 84.

nihilistic delusion: The *delusion* of nonexistence of the self, part of the self, or of some object in external reality.

norepinephrine: The neurohormone of the peripheral sympathetic nervous system. A *catecholamine* related to *epinephrine*. Also known as noradrenalin. See *biogenic amines*.

nosology: Science of classification of disorders, usually medical.

NREM sleep: See *sleep, Table of Sleep Disorders,* p. 84.

null hypothesis: See *Table of Research Terms,* p. 74.

nymphomania: See *-mania*.

107

O

object relations: The emotional bonds that exist between an individual and another person, as contrasted with his interest in, and love for, himself; usually described in terms of his capacity for loving and reacting appropriately to others.

obsession: A persistent, unwanted idea or impulse that cannot be eliminated by logic or reasoning.

obsessive compulsive neurosis: See *neurosis.*

obsessive compulsive personality: See *personality disorders.*

occupational psychiatry: A field of *psychiatry* concerned with the diagnosis and prevention of *mental illness* in industry, with the return of the psychiatric patient to work, and with psychiatric aspects of absenteeism, *accident proneness*, personnel policies, operational fatigue, vocational adjustment, retirement, and related phenomena.

occupational therapy: An adjunctive therapy that utilizes purposeful activities as a means of altering the course of illness. The patient's relationship to staff personnel and to other patients in the occupational therapy setting is often more therapeutic than the activity itself.

Oedipus complex: Attachment of the child to the parent of the opposite sex, accompanied by envious and *aggressive* feelings toward the parent of the same sex. These feelings are largely *repressed* (i.e. made *unconscious*) because of the fear of displeasure

108

or punishment by the parent of the same sex. In its original use, the term applied only to the boy or man.

oligophrenia: *Mental retardation.*

onanism: Incomplete sexual relations with withdrawal just prior to ejaculation. Coitus interruptus. Incorrectly used as a synonym for *masturbation.*

ontogenetic: Pertaining to the development of the individual. Distinguished from *phylogenetic.*

open hospital: A mental hospital, or section thereof, that has no locked doors or other forms of physical restraint.

operant conditioning: See *behavior therapy, biofeedback.*

oral phase: See *psychosexual development.*

organic brain syndrome: Any *mental disorder* associated with or caused by disturbance in the physiologic functioning of brain tissue at any level of organization—structural, hormonal, biochemical, electrical, etc.; also known as the acute and chronic *brain disorders* (in DSM-I), the *organic reaction type, organic psychosis.*

The organic brain syndromes are contrasted with the functional psychoses (see *functional*). Such dichotomization tends to obscure the fact that there is no single organic syndrome, but rather a range of several, and incorrectly suggests that there is a one-to-one relationship between the extent of the organic involvement and the type and severity of the associated mental symptoms. In actuality, the syndrome is a composite of many factors—the patient's genetic and constitutional endowments, the personality and character developed during a lifetime of experience, the current conflicts the patient faces regardless of origin, the immediate environment together with the organic changes in the *central nervous system.*

In any particular case, one or more of the following characteristic symptoms may be predominant (see also *mental status*): (1) disturbances in consciousness and level of attention; (2) disturbances in *orientation*; (3) impairment of memory; (4) impairment in other intellectual functions, including general knowledge, counting and calculation, comprehension, ability to learn, ability to plan, *abstraction ability*, general efficiency of perform-ance; (5) personality changes, often including an intensification of character traits that, at least retrospectively, can be recognized as part of the premorbid makeup, and frequently traits and conduct that are out of keeping with the premorbid makeup.

Some *psychiatrists* make a distinction between the symptomatic psychoses and the organic *dementias*. The symptomatic or exog-enous psychoses are those disturbances, usually acute in nature and reversible, related to disease processes outside the central nervous system, such as toxic and infectious diseases, systemic, visceral, metabolic and endocrine disorders, pregnancy and the puerperium. The term 'organic' is then reserved for those mental disturbances accompanying a demonstrable central nervous system lesion (e.g. head trauma, central nervous system infection, develop-mental degenerative disease or tumor), with the implication that the condition is chronic and, even if not progressive, is not wholly reversible.

The symptomatic psychoses were called acute brain disorders in *DSM-I*. They can be subdivided into two types:

  a) acute confusional state—with confusion (*disorientation*), clouding of consciousness (frequently shifting in degree, from preoccupation to *stupor* to *coma*), and disturbances in im-mediate and recent memory, in a setting of *anxiety* or per-plexity and agitation;

  b) *delirium*—added to the symptoms of the acute confusional state are such secondary elaborations as *hallucinations* (especially visual) and *delusions*.

The chronic brain disorders of DSM-I corresponded to the or-ganic *dementias* of other classifications; they have also been termed the endogenous psychoses. They are chronic, irreversible, and characterized by progressive deterioration.

organic disease: A disease characterized by demonstrable structural or biochemical abnormality in an organ or tissue. Sometimes im-precisely used as an antonym for *functional disorder*.

organic psychosis, organic reaction: See *organic brain syndrome*.

orgasm: The perception of a peak reaction to sexual stimulation accompanied by a release of sexual tension. This complex psychophysiologic response is normally accompanied by ejaculation of semen in the man and spasmodic muscular contractions, particularly in the genital area, in both sexes. Changes in muscle tone and *autonomic nervous system* activity take place throughout the body.

orgasmic dysfunction: Inability of the woman to achieve *orgasm* through physical stimulation. Masters and Johnson describe two types. In primary orgasmic dysfunction the woman has never had an orgasm through any physical contact including *masturbation*. In situational orgasmic dysfunction there has been at least one instance of orgasm through physical contact.

orientation: Awareness of one's self in relation to time, place, and person.

orthomolecular treatment (megavitamin therapy): Literally, the straightening of twisted molecules. A treatment based on the assumption that for every twisted mind there is a twisted molecule and that in some way psychiatric illness, and perhaps other illnesses, are due to biochemical abnormalities resulting in increased needs for specific substances such as vitamins. Initially orthomolecular treatment involved very large doses of vitamin B_3 (nicotinic acid or nicotinamide) for the treatment of *schizophrenia*. Later it included the use of nicotinamide adenine dinucleotide (NAD), the co-enzyme derived from vitamin B_3. Over the years it has evolved to include ascorbic acid, folic acid, vitamin B_{12} and other vitamins, hormones, diets, and drugs. The exact chemicals used vary from one clinician to another. This variable treatment is of unknown and unproven efficacy.

orthopsychiatry: An approach to the study and treatment of human behavior that involves the collaborative effort of *psychiatry*, *psychology*, psychiatric social work, and other behavioral, medical, and social sciences in the study and treatment of human behavior in the clinical setting. Emphasis is placed on preventive techniques to promote healthy emotional growth and development, particularly of children.

Otis Quick Scoring Mental Abilities Test: See *Table of Psychological Tests*, p. 78.

111

outreach: See *community mental health center.*

overcompensation: A *conscious* or *unconscious* process in which a real or imagined physical or psychologic deficit inspires exaggerated correction. Introduced by *Adler.*

overdetermination: A term indicating the multiple causes of a single emotional reaction or symptom. Thus, a single symptom expresses the confluence and condensation of *unconscious drives* and needs as well as the *defenses* against them.

P

pandemic: See under *epidemiology.*

panphobia: See *phobia.*

paranoia: See *paranoid states.*

paranoid: An adjective applied to individuals who are overly suspicious.

paranoid personality: See *personality disorders.*

paranoid states: *Psychotic* disorders in which a *delusion*, generally persecutory or grandiose, is the essential abnormality and accounts for disturbances in mood, behavior, and thinking (including *hallucinations*) that may be present. Its two major subdivisions are:

   involutional paranoid state (involutional paraphrenia): A paranoid psychosis characterized by delusion formation that begins in the involutional period. Distinguished from *schizophrenia, paranoid type,* by the absence of schizophrenic thought disorder.

paranoia: An extremely rare condition characterized by the gradual development of an intricate, complex, and elaborate paranoid system of thinking based on (and often proceeding logically from) misinterpretation of an actual event. Frequently the individual considers himself endowed with unique and superior ability. In spite of a chronic course, this condition does not seem to interfere with the rest of the individual's thinking and personality. To be distinguished from *schizophrenia, paranoid type.*

paraphrenia: A paranoid state consisting of a persecutory or grandiose *delusional* system of thinking without the primary disturbances of thinking and *affect* that characterize *schizophrenia, paranoid type.* See also *involutional paranoid state* under *paranoid states.*

parapraxis: A faulty act, blunder or lapse of memory such as a slip of the tongue or misplacement of an article. According to *Freud,* these acts are caused by *unconscious* motives.

paraprofessional: See *allied health professional.*

parapsychology: The study of sensory and motor phenomena shown by some human beings (and some animals, it appears) that occur without the mediation of the known sensory and motor organs. The data of parapsychology are not accounted for by the tenets of conventional science whose advocates believe that man cannot communicate without his sensory organs, nor move physical objects without using his known motor organs in some way. See also *metapsychiatry, metapsychology.*

parasympathetic nervous system: That part of the *autonomic nervous system* that controls the life-sustaining organs of the body under normal, danger-free conditions. See *sympathetic nervous system.*

parataxic distortion: H. S. Sullivan's term for certain distortions in judgment and perception, particularly in interpersonal relations, based upon the observer's need to perceive subjects and relationships in accordance with a pattern set by earlier experience. Parataxic distortions develop as a *defense* against *anxiety*. See *Sullivan*.

paresis: Weakness of organic origin; incomplete paralysis; term often used instead of *general paresis*.

paresthesia: Abnormal tactile sensation. Often described as burning, pricking, tickling, tingling, or creeping. May be *hallucinatory* in certain *psychoses* or a manifestation of neurological disease.

Parkinsonian syndromes: A group of basal ganglia diseases characterized by one or more of the following clinical pictures: involuntary tremors, rigidity of muscles, *bradykinesia*. See *extrapyramidal syndrome*.

partial hospitalization: A psychiatric treatment program for patients who require hospitalization but not on a full-time basis. For example:

> **day hospital:** A special facility or an arrangement within a hospital setting that enables the patient to come to the hospital for treatment during the day and return home at night.

> **night hospital:** A hospital or hospital service for patients who are able to work or otherwise function in the community during the day but who require specialized treatment and supervision in a hospital setting after working hours.

> **weekend hospital:** A hospital setting providing a treatment program over weekends. The patient resumes his usual work and activities outside the hospital during the week.

See also *community mental health center*.

passive-aggressive personality: See *personality disorders*.

passive-dependent personality: A disorder manifested by marked indecisiveness, emotional dependency, and lack of self-confidence. For diagnostic purposes, considered to be a subtype of *passive-aggressive personality*. See *personality disorders*.

pastoral counseling: The use of psychological principles by trained clergymen in interviews with parishioners who seek help with emotional problems.

pathognomonic: A medical term applied to a symptom or group of symptoms that are specifically diagnostic or typical of a disease entity.

Pavlov, Ivan Petrovich (1849–1936): Russian neurophysiologist noted for his research in *conditioning*. Awarded Nobel Prize in Medicine (1904) for his work on the physiology of digestion.

Pavlovian conditioning: See *conditioning* under *behavior therapy*.

pavor nocturnus (night terrors): See *Table of Sleep Disorders*, p. 84.

pederasty: *Homosexual* anal intercourse between men and boys as the passive partners. The term is used less precisely to denote male homosexual anal intercourse.

pedophilia: A *sexual deviation* involving sexual activity of adults with children as the objects. It may involve any form of heterosexual or *homosexual* intercourse.

peer review: Review of services rendered by physicians by panels of their "peers" or other physicians. See also *Professional Standards Review Organization*, and *utilization review committee*.

pellagra: A specific vitamin B_3 (nicotinamide) deficiency that manifests major mental symptoms such as *delusions* and impaired thinking, and also diarrhea and dermatitis. It is correctable by treatment with vitamin B_3.

penis envy: In psychoanalytic psychology, envy by the woman of the man. More generally, the woman's wish for the man's attributes.

period prevalence: See *Table of Research Terms*, p. 74.

perseveration: See *Table of Neurologic Deficits*, p. 72.

persona: A Jungian term for the personality "mask" or facade that each person presents to the outside world. Distinguished from the person's inner being or *anima*. See *Jung*.

personality: The characteristic way in which a person behaves; the ingrained pattern of behavior that each person evolves, both *consciously* and *unconsciously*, as his style of life or way of being in adapting to his environment. See *adaptation, character disorder, personality disorders*.

115

personality disorders: A group of mental disorders characterized by deeply ingrained maladaptive patterns of behavior, generally life-long in duration and consequently often recognizable by the time of *adolescence* or earlier. Affecting primarily the *personality* of the individual, they are different in quality from *neurosis* and *psychosis*.

antisocial personality: A personality disorder characterized by a basic lack of socialization and by behavior patterns that bring the individual repeatedly into conflict with society. People with this disorder are incapable of significant loyalty to individuals, groups, or social values and are grossly selfish, callous, irresponsible, impulsive, and unable to feel guilt or to learn from experience and punishment. Frustration tolerance is low. Such individuals tend to blame others or offer plausible rationalizations for their behavior.

asthenic personality: A personality disorder characterized by easy fatigability, low energy level, lack of enthusiasm, marked incapacity for enjoyment, and over-sensitivity to physical and emotional stress.

cyclothymic personality (affective personality). A personality disorder characterized by recurring and alternating periods of *depression* and elation not readily attributable to external circumstances.

explosive personality: A personality disorder characterized by gross outbursts of rage or of verbal or physical aggressiveness. Outbursts are strikingly different from the individual's usual behavior, and he may be regretful and repentant for them. See *aggression*.

hysterical personality (histrionic personality disorder): A personality disorder characterized by excitability, emotional instability, over-reactivity, and self-dramatization that is attention-seeking and often seductive, whether or not the individual is aware of its purpose. Often individuals with this disorder are immature, self-centered, vain, and unusually dependent on others.

inadequate personality: A personality disorder characterized by ineffectual responses to emotional, social, intellectual, and physical demands. While the individual seems neither physically nor mentally deficient, he does manifest inadaptibility, ineptness, poor judgment, social instability, and lack of physical and emotional stamina.

obsessive compulsive personality (anankastic personality): A personality disorder characterized by excessive concern with conformity and adherence to standards of *conscience*. Individuals with this disorder may be rigid, overinhibited, overconscientious, overdutiful, indecisive, perfectionistic, and unable to relax easily.

paranoid personality: A personality disorder characterized by hypersensitivity, rigidity, unwarranted suspicion, jealousy, envy, excessive self-importance, and a tendency to blame others and ascribe evil motives to them.

passive-aggressive personality: A personality disorder characterized by aggressive behavior manifested in passive ways, such as obstructionism, pouting, procrastination, intentional inefficiency, or stubbornness. The *aggression* often arises from resentment at failing to find gratification in a relationship with an individual or institution upon which the individual is overdependent.

schizoid personality: A personality disorder manifested by shyness, over-sensitivity, seclusiveness, frequent daydreaming, avoidance of close or competitive relationships, and often eccentricity. Individuals with this condition often react to disturbing experiences and conflicts with apparent detachment and are often unable to express hostility and ordinary aggressive feelings.

persuasion: A therapeutic approach based on direct suggestion and guidance intended to influence favorably patients' attitudes, behaviors, and goals.

perversion: An imprecise term used loosely to designate sexual variance.

petit mal: See *epilepsy*.

phallic phase: See *psychosexual development*.

phantom limb: A phenomenon frequently experienced by amputees, in which sensations, often painful, appear to originate in the amputated extremity.

phenomenology: The study of occurrences or happenings in their own right, rather than from the point of view of inferred causes; specifically, the theory that behavior is determined, not by external reality as it can be described objectively in physical terms, but rather by the way in which the subject perceives that reality at any moment. See *existentialism.*

phenothiazine derivatives: A group of *psychotropic* drugs that, chemically, have in common the phenothiazine configuration but that differ from one another through variations in chemical radicals. As a group of drugs the phenothiazines are also known as *antipsychotic drugs.* See *Table of Drugs Used in Psychiatry,* p. 68.

phenotype: The observable attributes of an individual; the physical manifestations of his *genotype.*

phenylketonuria (PKU): A genetic metabolic disturbance characterized by an inability to convert phenylalanine to tyrosine. Results in the abnormal accumulation of chemicals that interfere with brain development. Treatable by diet when detected in infancy. Detectable by a blood test for the presence of phenylpyruvic acid. If untreated, *mental retardation* results. Also known as phenylpyruvic oligophrenia.

phenylpyruvic oligophrenia: See *phenylketonuria (PKU).*

phobia: An *obsessive,* persistent, unrealistic intense *fear* of an object or situation. The fear is believed to arise through a process of displacing an internal (*unconscious*) conflict to an external object symbolically related to the conflict. See also *displacement.* Some of the common phobias are:

    acrophobia: Fear of heights.
    agoraphobia: Fear of open places.
    ailurophobia: Fear of cats.
    algophobia: Fear of pain.
    claustrophobia: Fear of closed spaces.
    erythrophobia: Fear of blushing; sometimes used to refer to the blushing itself.
    mysophobia: Fear of dirt and germs.
    panphobia: Fear of everything.
    xenophobia: Fear of strangers.

phobic neurosis: See under *neurosis.*

phrenology: Theory of relationship between bony structure of the skull and mental traits.

phylogenetic: Pertaining to the development of the species. Distinguished from *ontogenetic.*

physiologic self-regulation: See *biofeedback.*

Piaget, Jean (1896-): Swiss *psychologist* noted for his theoretical concepts of and research on the mental development of children. See *cognitive development.*

piblokto: see *culture specific syndromes.*

pica: The craving and eating of unusual foods or non-food substances. Seen in pregnancy, emotional disturbances in children, and *psychoses.*

Pick's disease: A presenile degenerative disease of the brain, possibly hereditary, affecting the cerebral cortex focally, particularly the frontal lobes. Symptoms include intellectual deterioration, emotional instability, and loss of social adjustment. See *Alzheimer's disease.*

Pickwickian syndrome: See *Table of Sleep Disorders,* p. 84.

Pinel, Phillipe (1746-1826): French physician-reformer who pioneered in abolishing the use of restraints in the care of the mentally ill.

piperidine: See *Table of Drugs Used in Psychiatry,* p. 68.

piperazine: See *Table of Drugs Used in Psychiatry,* p. 68.

PKU: See *phenylketonuria.*

placebo: Originally, an inactive substance such as a "bread pill" given to placate a patient who demands medication that is not necessary. Useful in research and practice because of its potential psychological effect, which may be neutral, therapeutic, or noxious depending on suggestion by the therapist or experimenter and the patient's own expectations, faith, *fear,* apprehension, or hostility. In British usage a placebo is sometimes called a **dummy.**

119

play therapy: A treatment technique utilizing the child's play as a medium for expression and communication between patient and therapist.

pleasure principle: The *psychoanalytic* concept that man instinctually seeks to avoid pain and discomfort and strives for gratification and pleasure. In personality development theory the pleasure principle antedates and subsequently comes in conflict with the *reality principle.*

point prevalence: See *Table of Research Terms,* p. 74.

polyphagia: Pathological overeating. Also known as *bulimia.*

porphyria: A metabolic disorder characterized by the excretion of prophyrins in the urine and accompanied by attacks of abdominal pain, peripheral neuropathy, and a variety of mental symptoms. Some types are precipitated by barbiturates and alcohol.

postpartum psychosis: Any *psychosis* occurring within a fixed period (approximately 90 days) after childbirth. It may be associated with severe *depression* or symptoms of *schizophrenia.*

potency: The male's ability to carry out sexual relations. Often used to refer specifically to the capacity to have and maintain adequate erection of the penis during sexual intercourse. See *impotence.*

practice effects: See *Table of Research Terms,* p. 74.

preconscious: Referring to thoughts that are not in immediate awareness but that can be recalled by *conscious* effort.

pregenital: In *psychoanalysis,* refers to the period of early childhood before the genitals have begun to exert the predominant influence in the organization or patterning of sexual behavior. Oral and anal influences predominate during this period. See *psychosexual development.*

premature ejaculation: Ejaculation occurring immediately before sexual intercourse or very early in sexual intercourse. The rapidity of ejaculation prevents the woman from achieving sexual satisfaction or reaching *orgasm.* This occasionally can be a normal occurrence such as in the early excitement phase of a relationship, particularly in younger men, but assumes clinical significance when it is frequent enough to be an established pattern of response which leads to sexual frustration of either or both partners.

pressured speech: Rapid, accelerated, frenzied speech. Sometimes it exceeds the ability of the vocal musculature to articulate, leading to jumbled and cluttered speech; at other times it exceeds the ability of the listener to comprehend as the speech expresses a *flight of ideas* (as in *mania*) or an unintelligible jargon.

prevalence: See *Table of Research Terms*, p. 74.

prevention (preventive psychiatry): In traditional medical usage, the prevention or prophylaxis of a disorder. The modern trend, particularly in *community psychiatry*, is to broaden the meaning of prevention to encompass also the amelioration, control, and limitation of disease. Prevention is often categorized as follows:
    primary prevention: Measures to prevent a *mental disorder* (e.g. by nutrition, substitute parents, etc.).
    secondary prevention: Measures to limit a disease process (e.g. through early case finding and treatment).
    tertiary prevention: Measures to reduce impairment or disability following a disorder (e.g. through *rehabilitation* programs).

primal scene: In *psychoanalytic* theory, the real or fancied observation by the infant of parental or other heterosexual intercourse.

primary gain: The relief from emotional *conflict* and the freedom from *anxiety* achieved by a *defense mechanism*. The concept is that mental states, both normal and pathological, develop defensively in largely *unconscious* attempts to cope with or to resolve unconscious conflicts. All *mental mechanisms* operate in the service of the primary gain, and the need for such gain may be thought of as responsible for the initiation of an emotional illness. To be distinguished from *secondary gain*.

primary process: In *psychoanalytic* theory, the generally unorganized mental activity characteristic of *unconscious* mental life. Seen in less disguised form in infancy and in dreams. It is marked by the free discharge of energy and excitation without regard to the demands of environment, reality, or logic. See *secondary process*.

primitive therapy: Treatment in non-literate societies for medical

121

disorders using magical and religious principles, but at times also things which are empirically effective, such as herbs, e.g.: rauwolfia.

Prince, Morton (1854-1929): American *psychiatrist* and *neurologist* known for his work on *multiple personalities*.

prison psychosis: See *Ganser's syndrome*.

privilege: See *Table of Legal Terms*, p. 70.

privileged communication: See *Table of Leal Terms*, p. 70.

problem oriented record: A simple conceptual framework to expedite and improve the medical record. The record is structured to contain four logically sequenced sections: (1) the data base, (2) the problem list, (3) plans, and (4) follow-up. The data base provides the information required for each patient regardless of diagnosis or presenting problems. The problem list is the list of numbered problems characterizing the patient to be treated. The plans specify what is to be done with regard to each problem, including what further needs to be done to identify and delineate the problem, what treatments are to be enacted for each problem and what education of the patient and family is to be conducted regarding his problems. Plans are specified for each problem separately. Follow-up includes progress notes and often flow sheets. Progress notes are titled by problem title and numbered according to their number on the problem list. Each progress note is subdivided into a data section (differentiated by data source—subjective and objective), assessments of the data entered concerning the problem, and plans for the problem as it has been assessed.

process schizophrenia: See *schizophrenia*.

Professional Standards Review Organization (PSRO): An organization of physicians (or in some cases *allied health professionals*) in a designated region, state, or community to review the quality of health care services. A basic intent is to ensure that health care services rendered are "medically necessary", particularly in the case of inpatient hospital services which might, upon review, be adjudged more effectively rendered on an ambulatory basis or in another health care facility. Specifically required by federal law (PL 92-603, Social Security Amendments of 1972) in relation to

122

hospital care under *Medicare* and Medicaid, but may later be extended to out of hospital care.

projection: A *defense mechanism*, operating *unconsciously*, whereby that which is emotionally unacceptable in the self is unconsciously rejected and attributed (projected) to others.

projective tests: Psychological tests used as a diagnostic tool in which the test material is so unstructured that any response will reflect a projection of some aspect of the subject's underlying *personality* and *psychopathology*. See *Table of Psychological Tests*, p. 78.

prosopagnosia: See *Table of Neurologic Deficits*, p. 72.

pseudofamily: See *caregiver*.

PSRO: See *Professional Standards Review Organization*.

psychasthenia: Obsolete term introduced by *Janet* to include *obsessions, compulsions*, doubts, feelings of inadequacy, and *phobias*. See *neurasthenia*.

psyche: The mind.

psychedelic: A term applied to any of several drugs that may induce *hallucinations* and *psychotic states*, including the production of distortions of time, sound, color, etc. Among the more commonly used psychedelics are *LSD,* marijuana, *mescaline,* morning-glory seeds, psilocybin.

psychiatric illness: See *mental disorders*.

Psychiatric News: The official newspaper of the *American Psychiatric Association*. Published twice monthly.

psychiatric nurse: Generally, any nurse employed in a psychiatric hospital or other psychiatric setting, but ideally a nurse with special training and experience in the management of psychiatric patients. Sometimes the term is used to denote only those nurses who have a master's degree in psychiatric nursing. The psychiatric nurse is responsible for the planning and carrying out of well-formulated treatment plans for patients in a variety of settings including both chronic and acute psychiatric wards, day hospitals, and community facilities. May also serve as a psychiatric consultant to community agencies and as a primary therapist to individual patients or groups of patients, generally under appropriate psychiatric supervision.

psychiatrist: A licensed physician who specializes in the diagnosis, treatment, and prevention of mental and emotional disorders. His training generally encompasses a premedical university education, medical education leading to a medical degree, three or more years of approved residency training. For those who wish to enter a subspecialty such as child psychiatry, *psychoanalysis*, administration, and the like still other training is essential. See also *psychotherapy, medical.*

psychiatry: The medical science that deals with the origin, diagnosis, prevention, and treatment of *mental disorders.*

psychic determinism: See *determinism.*

psychic energizer: A popular term for drugs that stimulate or elevate the mood of a depressed patient. The preferred term is "antidepressant". See *Table of Drugs Used in Psychiatry*, p. 68.

psychoanalysis: A psychologic theory of the *psychology* of human development and behavior, a method of research, and a system of *psychotherapy*, originally developed by Sigmund *Freud.* Through analysis of *free associations* and *interpretation* of dreams, emotions and behavior are traced to the influence of *repressed instinctual drives* and *defenses* against them in the *unconscious*. Psychoanalytic treatment seeks to eliminate or diminish the undesirable effects of unconscious conflicts by making the patient aware of their existence, origin, and inappropriate expression in current emotions and behavior. See *Table of Schools of Psychiatry*, p. 77.

psychoanalyst: A person, usually a *psychiatrist*, who has had training in *psychoanalysis* and who employs the techniques of psychoanalytic therapy.

psychobiology: A school of psychiatric thought which views biological, psychological, and social life experiences of the individual as an integrated unit. Associated with Adolf *Meyer*, who introduced the term in the United States in 1915. See also *Table of Schools of Psychiatry*, p. 77.

psychodrama: A technique of *group psychotherapy* in which individuals express their own or assigned emotional problems in dramatization.

psychodynamics: The systematized knowledge and theory of human behavior and its motivation, the study of which depends largely upon the functional significance of emotion. Psychodynamics recognizes the role of *unconscious* motivation in human behavior. It is a predictive science, based on the assumption that a person's total make-up and probable reactions at any given moment are the product of past interactions between his specific *genetic* endowment and the environment in which he has lived since conception.

psychogenesis: Production or causation of a symptom or illness by mental or psychic factors as opposed to *organic* ones.

psychokinesis: The belief that directed thought processes can influence an event such as a throw of dice. See also *parapsychology* and *extrasensory perception (ESP)*.

psycholinguistics: The study of factors affecting activities involved in communicating and comprehending verbal information. See *kinesics*.

psychological tests: See *Table of Psychological Tests*, p. 78.

psychologist: One who has training in *psychology*. Generally holds a Ph.D. or M.A. degree.

psychologist, clinical: A *psychologist* with a graduate degree, usually a Ph.D., and with additional supervised training and experience in a clinical setting, who specializes in the evaluation and psychological amelioration of *mental disorders*. Frequently clinical psychologists work in medical settings in collaboration with *psychiatrists* and other physicians.

psychology: An academic discipline, a profession, and a science dealing with the study of mental processes and behavior in man and animals. See *psychiatry*.

psychology, analytic: See *analytic psychology* and *Jung*.

psychology, individual: See *individual psychology* and *Adler*.

psychometry: The science of testing and measuring mental and

125

psychologic ability, efficiency, potentials, and functioning, including *psychopathologic* components. See *Table of Psychological Tests*, p. 78.

psychomotor epilepsy: See *epilepsy*.

psychomotor excitement: Generalized physical and emotional over-activity in response to internal and/or external stimuli as in *hypomania*.

psychomotor retardation: A generalized slowing of physical and emotional reactions. The opposite of *psychomotor excitement*. See *depression*.

psychoneurosis: See *neurosis*.

psychoneurotic disorders: See *neurosis*.

psychopathic personality: An informal term for *anti-social personality*. Such individuals are sometimes referred to casually as "psycho-paths".

psychopathology: The study of the significant causes and processes in the development of *mental disorders*. Also the manifestations of mental disorders.

psychopharmacology: The study of the mental and behavioral effects of certain drugs. See *Table of Drugs Used in Psychiatry*, p. 68.

psychophysiologic disorders: A group of disorders characterized by physical symptoms that are caused by emotional factors and that involve a single organ system, usually under *autonomic nervous system* control. Symptoms are caused by physiological changes that normally accompany certain emotional states, but in these disorders the changes are more intense and sustained. Frequently called *psychosomatic* disorders. These disorders are usually named and classified according to the organ system involved (e.g., gastro-intestinal, respiratory).

psychosexual development: Generally, a term encompassing all of the influences from prenatal life onward including biological, cultural, and emotional that affect the sexuality of the individual throughout the life cycle. In *psychoanalysis* the term, more specifically, encompasses the various stages of libidinal maturation from infancy to

126

adulthood. The way in which the child experiences these stages significantly influences his basic personality characteristics in later life. The stages are:

oral phase: The earliest of the stages of infantile psychosexual development, lasting from birth to 12 months or longer. Usually subdivided into two stages: the oral *erotic*, relating to the pleasurable experience of sucking; and the oral *sadistic*, associated with aggressive biting. Both oral erotism and sadism continue into adult life in disguised and *sublimated* forms.

anal phase: The period of pregenital psychosexual development, usually from one to three years, in which the child has particular interest and concern with the process of defecation and the sensations connected with the anus. The pleasurable part of the experience is termed *anal erotism*. See also *anal character*.

phallic phase: The period from about two and a half to six years during which sexual interest, curiosity, and pleasurable experience center about the penis in boys, and in girls, to a lesser extent, the clitoris.

latency period: The period from about five to seven years to *adolescence* when there is an apparent cessation of psychosexual development.

genital phase: The culminating stage of development in which a person achieves a genuinely affectionate, mature relationship with a sex partner.

psychosis: A major *mental disorder* of organic or emotional origin in which the individual's ability to think, respond emotionally, remember, communicate, interpret reality, and behave appropriately is sufficiently impaired so as to interfere grossly with his capacity to meet the ordinary demands of life. Often characterized by regressive behavior, inappropriate mood, diminished impulse control, and such abnormal mental content as *delusions* and *hallucinations*. The term is applicable to conditions having a wide range of severity and duration. See *schizophrenia, manic-depressive psychosis, depression, involutional melancholia, organic brain syndrome,* and *reality testing*.

127

psychosocial development: The psychosocial progress of the individual beginning in infancy as primarily described by Erik *Erikson*. Specific developmental tasks involving social relations and the role of social reality are faced by the individual at phase-specific points in his development. The early tasks parallel stages of *psychosexual development;* the later tasks extend through adulthood. Successful and unsuccessful solutions to each task are listed below with the corresponding chronological period and psychosexual stage where applicable. See also *cognitive development.*

TASK SOLUTIONS	CHRONOLOGICAL PERIOD	PSYCHOSEXUAL STAGE
trust vs. mistrust	infancy	oral
autonomy vs. shame, doubt	early childhood (toddler)	anal
initiative vs. guilt	pre-school	phallic (oedipal)
industry vs. inferiority	school age	latency
identity vs. identity diffusion	adolescence	
intimacy vs. isolation	young adulthood	genital
generativity vs. self absorption	adulthood	
integrity vs. despair	mature age	

psychosomatic: Adjective to denote the constant and inseparable interaction of the *psyche* (mind) and the *soma* (body). Most commonly used to refer to illnesses in which the manifestations are primarily physical with at least a partial emotional *etiology.* See *psychophysiologic disorders.*

psychosurgery: Surgical intervention to sever fibers connecting one part of the brain with another or to remove or to destroy brain tissue with the intent of modifying or altering disturbances of behavior, thought content, or mood for which no organic pathological cause can be demonstrated by established tests and techniques. Also, such surgery may be undertaken for the relief of intractable pain.

psychotherapy: A generic term for the treatment of mental and

128

emotional disorders based primarily upon verbal or non-verbal communication with the patient. A major treatment method of *psychiatrists* and other physicians trained in psychiatric medicine (see *psychotherapy, medical*). Non-medical psychotherapy may be carried out by *psychologists, social workers,* nurses, *pastoral counselors,* and other professionals with special training in the technique. See *Table of Schools of Psychiatry,* p. 77.

psychotherapy, medical: A medical procedure carried out by a physician trained in psychiatric medicine to treat mental, emotional, and *psychosomatic* illness through a relationship with the patient in an individual, group, or family setting. Medical psychotherapy always entails continuing medical diagnostic evaluation and responsibility and may be carried out in conjunction with drug and other physical treatments. Medical psychotherapy subsumes that the psychological and physical components of an illness are intertwined and that at any point in the disease process, psychological symptoms may give rise to, substitute for, or run concurrently with physical symptoms, and vice versa. Medical psychotherapy may encompass *psychoanalysis,* insight-oriented, *behavior,* re-educative, reconstructive, *family,* directive, supportive, and other forms of psychotherapy. See *Table of Schools of Psychiatry,* p. 77.

psychotic depressive reaction: A *psychosis* distinguished by a depressive mood attributed to some experience. See *depression.*

psychotomimetic: Literally, mimicking a *psychosis.* Used to refer to certain drugs such as *LSD (lysergic acid diethlyamide)* or *mescaline,* which produce psychotic states.

psychotropic: A term used to describe drugs that have a special action upon the *psyche.* See *Table of Drugs Used in Psychiatry,* p. 68.

puerperal psychosis: See *postpartum psychosis.*

punishment techniques: See *aversive control* under *behavior therapy.*

pyromania: See *-mania.*

129

Q

q-sort: See *Table of Research Terms,* p. 74.

R

random sample: See *Table of Research Terms,* p. 74.

Rank, Otto (1884-1939): Viennese lay *psychoanalyst* and early follower of *Freud.* In 1924 his book *The Trauma of Birth* was published. Emigrated to the United States in 1935. Strongly influenced the Philadelphia Child Guidance Center and the University of Pennsylvania School of Social Work.

rapport: The feeling of harmonious accord, mutual responsiveness, and *sympathy* that contributes to the patient's confidence in the therapist and willingness to work cooperatively with him. To be distinguished from *transference,* which is *unconscious.*

rationalization: A *defense mechanism,* operating *unconsciously,* in which the individual attempts to justify or make *consciously* tolerable, by plausible means, feelings, behavior and motives that would otherwise be intolerable. Not to be confused with conscious evasion or dissimulation. See *projection*.

Ray, Isaac (1807-1881): A founder of the *American Psychiatric Association* whose *Treatise on the Medical Jurisprudence of Insanity* was the pioneer American work in this field.

reaction formation: A *defense mechanism*, operating *unconsciously*, wherein attitudes and behavior are adopted that are the opposites of impulses the individual harbors either *consciously* or unconsciously (e.g. excessive moral zeal may be a reaction to strong but *repressed* asocial impulses).

reactive depression: See *depression*. This term has been replaced by depressive neurosis. See under *neurosis*.

reactive schizophrenia: See *schizophrenia*.

reality principle: In *psychoanalytic* theory, the concept that the *pleasure principle*, which represents the claims of *instinctual* wishes, is normally modified by the inescapable demands and requirements of the external world. In fact, the reality principle may still work in behalf of the pleasure principle; but it reflects compromises in the nature of the gratification and allows for the postponement of gratification to a more appropriate time. The reality principle usually becomes more prominent in the course of development but may be weak in certain psychiatric illnesses and undergo strengthening during treatment.

reality testing: The ability to evaluate the external world objectively and to differentiate adequately between it and the internal world, between self and non-self. Falsification of reality, as with massive *denial* or *projection*, indicates a severe disturbance of *ego* functioning and/or the perceptual and memory processes upon which it is partly based. See *psychosis*.

recall: The process of bringing a memory into *consciousness*. Recall is often used to refer to the recollection of facts, events, and feelings that have occurred in the immediate past.

reciprocal inhibition and desensitization: See *behavior therapy*.

reference, delusion of (idea of): See *ideas of reference.*

regression: The partial or symbolic return to more infantile patterns of reacting. Manifested in a wide variety of circumstances such as normal sleep, play, severe physical illness, and in many *mental disorders.*

rehabilitation: The methods and techniques used in a program that seeks to achieve maximal function and optimal adjustment for the identified patient, and to prevent relapses or recurrences of his condition (because of the latter, sometimes termed tertiary *prevention*). The focus in rehabilitation is on the patient's assets and recoverable functions, rather than on the liabilities engendered by his pathology or the complications of disuse and social deterioration which formerly were often mistakenly considered to be part of the underlying disease process. Includes individual and *group psychotherapy*, directed socialization, vocational retraining, education. See *community psychiatry.*

Reich, Wilhelm (1897-1957): German *psychoanalyst* who emigrated to the United States in 1939; noted for his emphasis on the necessity of the free expression of sexual *libido* ("orgone") as a cure for the *neuroses.*

reinforcement: See under *behavior therapy.*

reinforcer: See *reinforcement* under *behavior therapy.*

reinforcing stimulus: See *reinforcement* under *behavior therapy.*

relative risk: See *Table of Research Terms*, p. 74.

reliability: See *Table of Research Terms*, p. 74.

REM sleep: See *sleep.*

remission: Abatement of an illness.

remotivation: A group treatment technique administered by nursing service personnel in a mental hospital; of particular value to long-term, withdrawn patients by way of stimulating their communication skills and interest in their environment.

repetition compulsion: In *psychoanalytic* theory the impulse to reenact earlier emotional experiences. Considered by *Freud* more fundamental than the *pleasure principle*. According to Ernest *Jones*: "The blind impulse to repeat earlier experiences and situations quite irrespective of any advantage that doing so might bring from a pleasure-pain point of view."

repression: A *defense mechanism*, operating *unconsciously*, that banishes unacceptable ideas, *affects*, or *impulses*, from *consciousness* or that keeps out of consciousness what has never been conscious. Although not subject to voluntary recall, the repressed material may emerge in disguised form. Often confused with the conscious mechanism of *suppression*.

reserpine: See *Table of Drugs Used in Psychiatry*, p. 68.

resident: A physician who is in graduate training to qualify as a specialist in a particular field of medicine, such as *psychiatry*. The American Board of Psychiatry and Neurology requires three years of psychiatric residency training in an approved hospital or clinic to qualify for examination.

resistance: The individual's *conscious* or *unconscious psychological defense* against bringing *repressed* (unconscious) thoughts to light. See *mental mechanism*.

respondent conditioning: See *conditioning* under *behavior therapy*.

retardation: Slowing down of mental and physical activity. Most frequently seen in severe *depressions,* which are sometimes spoken of as retarded depressions. Not the same as *mental retardation*.

retrograde amnesia: See *amnesia*.

retrospective falsification: *Unconscious* distortion of past experiences to conform to present emotional needs.

ribonucleic acid (RNA): A vital nucleic acid manufactured by *DNA (desoxyribonucleic acid)*. Essential for the building of body proteins from amino acids. Appears to play a key role in memory.

right to treatment: See *Table of Legal Terms*, p. 70.

rigidity: An individual's excessive resistance to change. See also *Parkinsonian syndromes*.

ritual: Any psychomotor activity sustained by an individual to relieve

133

anxiety. Most commonly seen in *obsessive compulsive neurosis*. See *neurosis*.

RNA: See *ribonucleic acid*.

Romberg's sign: See *Table of Neurologic Deficits*, p. 72.

Rorschach test: See *Table of Psychological Tests*, p. 78.

Rush, Benjamin (1745-1813): Early American physician, signer of the Declaration of Independence, and author of the first American text on *psychiatry* (1812). He is called "the father of American psychiatry".

S

sadism: Pleasure derived from inflicting physical or psychological pain or abuse on others. The sexual significance of sadistic wishes or behavior may be *conscious* or *unconscious*. When necessary for sexual gratification, classifiable as a *sexual deviation*.

satyriasis: Pathologic or exaggerated sexual drive or excitement in the man. May be of psychic or organic *etiology*. See *nymphomania*.

schedule of reinforcement: See *reinforcement* under *behavior therapy*.

schizoid personality: See *personality disorders*.

schizophrenia: A large group of disorders, usually of *psychotic* proportion, manifested by characteristic disturbances of thought, mood, and behavior. Thought disturbances are marked by alterations of concept formation that may lead to misinterpretation of reality and sometimes to *delusions* and *hallucinations*. Mood changes include *ambivalence*, constriction, inappropriateness, and loss of *empathy* with others. Behavior may be withdrawn, *regressive*, and bizarre. Currently recognized types of schizophrenia are:

acute schizophrenic episode: A condition characterized by the acute onset of schizophrenic symptoms, often associated with confusion, perplexity, *ideas of reference*, emotional turmoil, excitement, *depression, fear*, or dream-like *dissociation*. This term is not applicable to acute episodes of the other types of schizophrenia described here.

catatonic type: A schizophrenic disorder manifested in either or both of two ways: by excessive and sometimes violent motor activity and excitement ("excited subtype") or by generalized inhibition manifested as *stupor, mutism, negativism*, or *waxy flexibility* ("withdrawn subtype").

childhood schizophrenia: Schizophrenia appearing before puberty. It is frequently manifested by *autism* and withdrawn behavior; failure to develop an *identity* separate from the mother's; and general unevenness, gross immaturity, and inadequacy in development.

chronic undifferentiated type: A condition manifested by definite signs of schizophrenic thought, *affect*, and behavior that are of a sufficiently mixed or indefinite type that they defy classification into one of the other types of schizophrenia.

hebephrenic type: A schizophrenic disorder characterized by disorganized thinking, shallow and inappropriate *affect*, inappropriate giggling, silly and *regressive* behavior and mannerisms, and frequent hypochondriacal complaints. *Delusions* and *hallucinations* are usually bizarre and not well organized.

latent type: A condition manifested by clear symptoms of schizophrenia but no history of psychotic schizophrenic episodes. Sometimes designated as incipient, pre-psychotic, pseudo-neurotic, pseudo-psychopathic, or *borderline* schizophrenia.

paranoid type: A schizophrenic disorder characterized primarily by the presence of persecutory or grandiose *delusions*, often associated with *hallucinations*.

135

process schizophrenia: Unofficial term for schizophrenia attributed more to organic factors than to environmental ones; typically begins gradually, continues chronically, and progresses (either rapidly or slowly) to an irreversible *psychosis*. See also *reactive schizophrenia,* to which this condition is contrasted.

reactive schizophrenia: Unofficial term for schizophrenia attributed primarily to strong predisposing and/or precipitating environmental factors; usually of rapid onset and brief duration, with the affected individual appearing well both before and after the schizophrenic episode. Differentiating this condition from *process schizophrenia* is generally considered more important in Europe than in this country.

residual type: A condition manifested by individuals with signs of schizophrenia who, following a psychotic schizophrenic episode, are no longer psychotic.

school phobia: A term used when a child, usually a pupil in the early elementary grades, unexpectedly and without apparent reason, strenuously refuses to attend school because of some irrational fear. The underlying *psychopathology* is believed to be an intense *separation anxiety* rooted in unresolved *dependency* ties.

schools of psychiatry: The various theoretical frames of reference that guide or form the rational basis for *psychiatrists'* formulations and methods of treatment. Typically, such formulations concentrate more on processes, such as *instincts* or stimulus-response patterns, than upon the total personality. Most commonly they are adduced to explain how psychiatric symptoms or disorders develop, how they interfere with functioning, and how and why they can be altered by therapeutic interventions. See *Table of Schools of Psychiatry,* p. 77, for an arbitrary listing of schools and their founders or leading proponents.

scotoma: A figurative blind spot in an individual's psychologic awareness. Also, a *neurologic* term indicating a visual defect.

screen memory: A *consciously* tolerable memory that serves as a cover or "screen" for another associated memory that would be disturbing and emotionally painful if recalled.

secondary gain: The external gain that is derived from any illness, such as personal attention and service, monetary gains, disability benefits, and release from unpleasant responsibility. See *primary gain.*

secondary process: In *psychoanalytic* theory, mental activity and thinking characteristic of the *ego* and influenced by the demands of the environment. Characterized by organization, systematization, *intellectualization,* and similar processes leading to logical thought and action in adult life. See also *primary process.*

sedative: A broad term applied to any agent that quiets or calms or allays excitement. The term is generally restricted to drugs that are not primarily used to achieve relief from *anxiety* or to induce *sleep.* See *Table of Drugs Used in Psychiatry,* p. 68.

senile dementia: A chronic *organic brain syndrome* associated with generalized atrophy of the brain due to aging. In addition to the organic symptoms present, self-centeredness, difficulty assimilating new experiences, and childish emotionality are usually prominent. Deterioration may range from minimal to severe.

sensitivity group: A group in which members strive to increase self-awareness and understanding of the group's dynamics, as distinct from treatment modalities that are designed to ameliorate emotional problems.

sensorium: Synonymous with consciousness. Includes the special sensory perceptive powers and their central correlation and integration in the brain. A clear sensorium conveys the presence of a reasonably accurate memory together with *orientation* for time, place, and person. See *mental status.*

sensory deprivation: The experience of being cut off from usual external stimuli and the opportunity for perception. May occur experimentally or accidentally in various ways such as through loss of hearing or eyesight, by becoming marooned, by solitary confinement, by assignment to a remote service post, or by travelling in space. May lead to disorganized thinking, *depression, panic, delusions,* and *hallucinations.*

sensory extinction: See *Table of Neurologic Deficits,* p. 72.

137

separation anxiety: The *fear* and apprehension noted in infants when removed from their mothers (or *surrogates*) or when approached by strangers. Most marked from sixth to tenth month. In later life, similar reaction may be caused by separation from significant persons or familiar surroundings.

serotonin: A neurotransmitter with an indole structure found both in peripheral ganglia and in the *central nervous system*. Its transmitter functions in the central nervous system are less clearly demonstrable than in the gastrointestinal tract. It is implicated indirectly in the psychobiology of both *schizophrenia* and *depression*. See also *biogenic amines*.

sexual deviation: The direction of sexual interest toward objects other than persons of the opposite sex, toward sexual acts not associated with coitus, or toward coitus performed under bizarre circumstances. See *bestiality, exhibitionism, fetishism, masochism, pedophilia, sadism, sodomy, transvestitism (transvestism), voyeurism*.

sexual orientation disturbance: An official diagnostic category for individuals whose sexual interests are directed primarily towards persons of the same sex and who are either disturbed by, in conflict with, or wish to change their sexual orientation. To be distinguished from *homosexuality* and *lesbianism*.

shaman: The original narrow definition is the term for healer in the Tungus tribe of northeastern Siberia. The broader use is as a practitioner whose ability comes from trance-like experience and inspiration from the supernatural spirits, as opposed to coming from systematic learning in an apprenticeship (Navaho "hand-trembler" as opposed to Navaho "medicine man"). The healer has a spirit-partner with whom he works in curing sick people.

shell shock: Obsolete term used in World War I to designate a wide variety of *psychotic* and *neurotic* disorders presumably due to combat experience. See *conversion, combat fatigue, hysterical neurosis, psychosis*.

shock treatment: A form of psychiatric treatment in which electric current, insulin, carbon dioxide, or Indoklon, is administered to the patient and results in a loss of consciousness or a convulsive or comatose reaction to alter favorably the course of the illness. Some common types of shock treatment are:

carbon dioxide treatment: A form of inhalation treatment in which carbon dioxide gas is administered to the point of *unconsciousness* in order to cause emotional *abreactions* and alleviation of *anxiety*.

electroconvulsive treatment (ECT): Use of electric current to induce *unconsciousness* and/or convulsive seizures. Most effective in the treatment of *depression*. Introduced by Cerletti and Bini in 1938. Modifications are electronarcosis, producing sleep-like states, and electrostimulation, which avoids convulsions. Used with anesthestics and muscle relaxants.

Indoklon treatment: A form of shock treatment in which a convulsive seizure is produced by intravenous injection or inhalation of the drug, Indoklon.

insulin coma treatment (ICT): A treatment primarily for *schizophrenia* in which insulin is injected in large enough doses to produce profound *hypoglycemia* (low blood sugar) resulting in *coma*. First used by Manfred Sakel in 1933. Its use in the United States has decreased since the introduction of *antipsychotic drugs*.

Metrazol shock treatment: A form of shock treatment, now rarely used, in which a convulsive seizure is produced by intravenous injection of Metrazol (known as Cardiazol in Europe). Introduced by L. von Meduna in 1934.

subcoma insulin treatment: A treatment in which insulin is administered to induce drowsiness or somnolence short of *coma*. Used to alleviate *anxiety*, stimulate appetite, and induce a feeling of well-being.

sibling: Term for a full brother or sister.

sibling rivalry: The competition between *siblings* for the love of a parent or for other recognition or gain.

simultanagnosia: See *Table of Neurologic Deficits*, p. 72.

situational depression: See *depressive neurosis* under *neurosis*.

139

Skinner, Burrhus Frederic (1904-   ): American *psychologist* noted for his research and writings on *operant conditioning*. Many of the procedures of *behavior therapy* are based on laboratory research by Skinner and his students.

sleep: The recurring periods of relative physical and psychological disengagement from one's environment known as sleep, are accompanied by characteristic EEG *(electroencephalogram)* findings and are divisible into two categories: non-rapid eye movement (NREM) sleep, also known as orthodox or synchronized (S) sleep and rapid eye movement (REM) sleep, also referred to as paradoxical or desynchronized (D) sleep. Dreaming sleep is another, though less accurate, term used for REM sleep.

Four stages of NREM sleep based on EEG findings are: Stage 1 occurring immediately after sleep begins with a pattern of low amplitude and fast frequency; Stage 2 having characteristic waves of 12-16 cycles per second known as sleep spindles; Stages 3 and 4 having progressive further slowing of frequency and increase in amplitude of the wave forms.

Over a period of about 1½ hours after the beginning of sleep, a person has progressed through the 4 stages of NREM sleep and emerges from them into the first period of REM sleep. REM sleep is associated with dreaming and brief cycles (20-30 minutes) of this sleep recur about every 90 minutes throughout the night. Coordinated rapid eye movements give this type of sleep its name.

Sleep patterns vary with age, state of health, medication and psychological state. See *Table of Sleep Disorders,* p. 84.

social breakdown syndrome: The concept that some of the mental patient's symptomatology is a result of treatment conditions and facilities and not a part of the primary illness. Factors bringing about this condition are: social labeling, learning the chronic sick role, atrophy of work and social skills, and *identification* with the sick. See *rehabilitation.*

social control: The way in which society or any of its subgroups, various institutions, organizations, and agencies exert influence upon the individual, or groups of individuals, to conform to the expectations and requirements of that society or subgroup. Control may be coercive (as by means of the law) or persuasive (through such devices as *suggestion*, blame, praise, reward, and recognition). See also *sociology*.

social psychiatry: The field of *psychiatry* concerned with the cultural, *ecologic*, and *sociologic* factors that engender, precipitate, intensify, prolong, or otherwise complicate maladaptive patterns of behavior and their treatment; sometimes used synonymously with *community psychiatry*, although the latter term should be limited to practical or clinical applications of social psychiatry. Important in social psychiatry is the *ecological* approach to maladaptive behavior, which is viewed not only as a deviation of an individual but also as a reflection of deviation in the social systems in which he lives.

social work: The use of community resources and of the *conscious* adaptive capacities of individuals and groups to better the adjustment of an individual to his environment and to improve the quality and functioning of an individual's external environment.

social worker, psychiatric: A social worker with specialized psychiatric training leading to a graduate degree (M.S.W. or D.S.W.) in social work. Such a worker may utilize all social work techniques such as case work, group work, and community organization in a psychiatric or mental health setting.

socialization: The process by which society integrates the individual and the way in which the individual learns to become a functioning member of that society. See *sociology*.

sociology: The study of the development and governing principles of social organization and the group behavior of people, in contrast to individual behavior. Overlaps to some extent with *cultural anthropology*. See also *alienation, social control, socialization*.

sociopath: An unofficial term for *antisocial personality*. See *personality disorders*.

sociotherapy: Any treatment in which emphasis is on socio-environmental and interpersonal rather than on *intrapsychic* factors, as in the *therapeutic community*. In most forms of sociotherapy, peer acceptance is an important element, typically achieved through confrontation by the group when peer expectations are not met.

141

sodomy: Anal intercourse. Legally, the term may include other types of perversion such as *bestiality*. See *sexual deviation*.

soma: The body.

somatic conversion: See *neurosis*.

somatization reactions: See *psychophysiologic disorders*.

somnambulism: See *Table of Sleep Disorders, sleep*, p. 84.

speech disturbance: Any disorder of verbal or nonverbal communication that is not due to faulty innervation of the speech muscles or organs of articulation. There is no single cause for any of the speech disturbances, but minimal cortical or subcortical dysfunction, including dysharmony in the physiologic predominance of one cerebral hemisphere over the other, may be an important factor in many patients. The term includes many language and *learning disabilities*. See *amimia* and *dyslexia*. See also *agraphia, aphasia* and *apraxia* in *Table of Neurologic Deficits*, p. 72.

standard deviation: See *Table of Research Terms*, p. 74.

Stanford-Binet Intelligence Scale: See *Table of Psychological Tests*, p. 78.

status epilepticus: Continuous epileptic seizures. See *epilepsy*.

stereotypy: Persistent mechanical repetition of speech or motor activity. Observed in *schizophrenia*.

stimulants: See *Table of Drugs Used in Psychiatry*, p. 68.

stimulus control: See under *behavior therapy*.

storefront: See *community mental health center*.

strephosymbolia: A tendency to reverse letters and words in reading and writing. Seen in *learning disability*.

stress reaction: See *gross stress reaction*.

stroke: Cerebrovascular accident (CVA); gross cerebral hemorrhage or softening of the brain following hemorrhage, thrombosis, or embolism of the cerebral arteries. Symptoms may include *coma*, paralysis (particularly on one side of the body), *convulsions*,

142

aphasia, and other neurologic signs determined by the location of the lesion.

stupor: A state in which the individual does not react to his surroundings and appears to be unaware of them. In catatonic stupor, the unawareness is more apparent than real. See *catatonic state.*

stuttering and stammering: Spasmodic speaking with involuntary halts and repetitions, usually considered *psychogenic.*

subcoma insulin treatment: See *shock treatment.*

subconscious: Obsolete term. Formerly used to include the *preconscious* (what can be recalled with effort) and the *unconscious.*

sublimation: A *defense mechanism,* operating *unconsciously,* by which *instinctual drives, consciously* unacceptable, are diverted into personally and socially acceptable channels.

substitution: A *defense mechanism,* operating *unconsciously,* by which an unattainable or unacceptable goal, *emotion,* or object is replaced by one that is more attainable or acceptable.

succinylcholine: A potent drug used intravenously in *anesthesia* as a skeletal muscle relaxant. Also used prior to electroconvulsive treatment to minimize the possibility of complications. See *shock treatment.*

suggestion: The process of influencing an individual to accept less critically an idea, belief, or attitude induced by the therapist.

Sullivan, Harry Stack (1892-1949): American *psychiatrist* and *psychoanalyst* known for his research in the *psychotherapy* of *schizophrenia* and for his view of complex interpersonal relationships as the basis of individual personality development.

superego: In *psychoanalytic* theory, that part of the *personality* structure associated with ethics, standards, and self-criticism. It is formed by the infant's *identification* with important and esteemed persons in his early life, particularly parents. The supposed or actual wishes of these significant persons are taken over as part of the child's own personal standards to help form the *conscience.* See *ego, id.*

143

supportive psychotherapy: A type of *psychotherapy* that aims to reinforce a patient's *defenses* and to help him suppress disturbing psychological material. Supportive psychotherapy utilizes such measures as inspiration, reassurance, *suggestion*, persuasion, counseling, and re-education. It avoids probing the patient's emotional *conflicts* in depth. See *psychotherapy*.

suppression: The *conscious* effort to control and conceal unacceptable impulses, thoughts, feelings, or acts.

surrogate: One who takes the place of another. In a child's growth and development, original affective attitudes and feelings towards a parent may in time be transferred to a *sibling*, a teacher, a relative, a friend. With each new surrogate there is less resemblance to the original attachment.

susto: See *culture specific syndromes*.

symbiosis: A mutually reinforcing relationship between two persons who are dependent on each other. A normal characteristic of the relationship between the mother and infant child.

symbiotic psychosis: A condition seen in 2-4 year old children with an abnormal relationship to a mothering figure. The *psychosis* is characterized by intense *separation anxiety*, severe *regression*, giving up of useful speech and *autism*.

symbolization: An *unconscious* mental process operating by *association* and based on similarity and *abstract* representation whereby one object or idea comes to stand for another through some part, quality, or aspect in which the two relate. The symbol carries in disguised form the emotional feelings vested in the initial object or idea.

sympathetic nervous system: That part of the *autonomic nervous system* that responds to dangerous or threatening situations by preparing the individual physiologically for "fight or flight". See *parasympathetic nervous system*.

sympathy: Compassion for another's *grief* or loss. To be differentiated from *empathy*.

symptom: A specific manifestation of a patient's condition indicative of an abnormal physical or mental state. Psychiatric symptoms are often the result of *unconscious conflict* and may represent in symbolic form an *instinctual* wish, the *defense* against such a wish, or a compromise between the two.

symptomatic psychoses: See *organic brain syndrome.*

syndrome: A configuration of *symptoms* that occur together and that constitute a recognizable condition. See, for example, *cri-du-chat, Gilles de la Tourette, Klinefelter's, Klüver-Bucy, Münchausen, Turner's, social breakdown, Wernicke-Korsakoff.*

syntactical (central) aphasia: See *Table of Neurological Deficits,* p. 72.

syphilis: A venereal disease, which, if untreated, may lead to *central nervous system* deterioration with *psychotic* manifestations in its later stages. See *general paralysis.*

systematic desensitization: See under *behavior therapy.*

T

tardive dyskinesia: Untoward effect, appearing after long term use of antipsychotic drugs with muscle involvement about the face, neck, and trunk, leading to spasms, *tics,* eye signs, and *speech disturbances.*

T-Group: A sensitivity training group. An educational technique in which a group of people meets regularly, usually with a specified leader, in order to learn about themselves, interpersonal relationships, group process and larger social systems. Its major aims include social effectiveness, interpersonal relatedness, and opening communication channels between the group member and others within one's social system. Sometimes called human relations groups.

talion law or principle: A primitive, unrealistic belief, usually *unconscious*, conforming to the Biblical injunction of an "eye for an eye" and a "tooth for a tooth". In *psychoanalysis*, the concept and fear that all injury, actual or intended, will be punished in kind— i.e. retaliated.

Tasks of Emotional Development (TED): See *Table of Psychological Tests*, p. 78.

TAT: *Thematic Apperception Test.* See *Table of Psychological Tests*, p. 78.

telepathy: The communication of thought from one person to another without the intervention of physical means. See *extrasensory perception, parapsychology.*

temporal lobe epilepsy: Psychomotor epilepsy. See *epilepsy.*

Thematic Apperception Test (TAT): See *Table of Psychological Tests*, p. 78.

therapeutic community: A term of British origin, now widely used, for a specially structured mental hospital milieu that encourages patients to function within the range of social norms.

thioxanthene derivatives: See *Table of Drugs Used in Psychiatry*, p. 68.

tic: An intermittent, involuntary, spasmodic movement of a group of muscles, often without a demonstrable external stimulus. A tic may be an expression of an emotional conflict or the result of *neurologic* disease.

token economy: See under *behavior therapy.*

toxic psychosis: A *psychosis* resulting from the poisonous effect of chemicals and drugs, and intrinsic metabolic states.

trainable: See *mental retardation.*

trance: A state of diminished activity and *consciousness* resembling *sleep.* Seen in *hypnosis, hysterical neurosis, dissociative type* (see under *neurosis*), and ecstatic religious states.

tranquilizer: A drug that decreases *anxiety* and *agitation,* usually without causing drowsiness. Preferred terms are antianxiety and antipsychotic drugs. See *Table of Drugs Used in Psychiatry,* p. 68.

transactional analysis: A *psychodynamic psychotherapy* that attempts to understand the interplay between therapist and patient—and ultimately between the patient and external reality—in terms of role theory, beginning with an exposure of current, well-defined, explicit roles, and ultimately evoking a recognition of implicit emotional roles and a repetition of earlier interactions that trace the genesis of current behavior. See *Table of Schools of Psychiatry,* p. 77.

transcendental meditation: See *biofeedback.*

transcultural psychiatry: See *cross cultural psychiatry.*

transference: The *unconscious* assignment to others of feelings and attitudes that were originally associated with important figures (parents, *siblings,* etc.) in one's early life. The transference relationship follows the pattern of its prototype. The *psychiatrist* utilizes this phenomenon as a therapeutic tool to help the patient understand his emotional problems and their origins. In the patient-physician relationship the transference may be negative (hostile) or positive (affectionate). See *countertransference,* and *parataxic distortion.*

transient situational disturbance: A transient disorder of any severity (including *psychosis*) that represents an acute reaction to overwhelming *stress,* such as the severe crying spells, loss of appetite, and social withdrawal of a child separated from its mother; or, in an adult, a reaction to an unwanted pregnancy manifested by suicidal gestures and hostile complaints. The symptoms generally recede as the stress diminishes.

transsexual: A disturbance of *gender identity* in which the person feels a lifelong discomfort with his or her own sex and a compelling desire to be of the opposite sex.

147

transvestitism (transvestism): Sexual pleasure derived from dressing or masquerading in the clothing of the opposite sex. The sexual origins of transvestitism may be *unconscious.* There is a strong wish to appear as a member of the opposite sex. Usually seen in men.

trauma: An extremely upsetting emotional experience that may aggravate or contribute to a *mental disorder.*

traumatic neuroses: The term encompasses neurotic reactions that have been attributed to or follow a situational traumatic event, or series of events, and includes combat, occupational, and *compensation neuroses.* The traumatic event may have some specific and symbolic emotional significance for the patient and may be reinforced by *secondary gain.*

trichotillomania: See *-mania.*

tricyclic derivatives: See *Table of Drugs Used in Psychiatry,* p. 68.

trisomy: The presence of three *chromosomes* instead of the two that normally represent each potential set of chromosomes. Humans have 23 pairs of chromosomes. A significant trisomy in *psychiatry* is that associated with *Down's syndrome.*

Tuke, William (1732-1822): English Quaker layman who pioneered in the treatment of patients without physical restraints.

Turner's syndrome: A *chromosomal* defect in women with a karyotype of XO and with 45 chromosomes rather than the usual 46. Clinical features of this disorder are small stature, webbed neck, abnormal ovarian development, and sometimes *mental retardation.*

type 1 error: See *Table of Research Terms,* p. 74.

type 2 error: See *Table of Research Terms,* p. 74.

U

ultradian rhythms: See *biological rhythms*.

unconditioned reflex (UCR): See *behavior therapy*.

unconditioned stimulus: See *stimulus control* under *behavior therapy*.

unconscious: That part of the mind or mental functioning of which the content is only rarely subject to awareness. It is a repository for data that have never been *conscious* (primary *repression*), or that may have become conscious briefly and later repressed (secondary repression).

undoing: A *defense mechanism*, operating *unconsciously*, in which something unacceptable and already done is symbolically *acted out* in reverse, usually repetitiously, in the hope of relieving *anxiety*.

unipolar psychosis: An *affective disorder* that is characterized more often by recurrent *depressions*, and less frequently by recurrent manic states. Contrast with *bipolar psychosis*. See also *manic-depressive psychosis*.

utilization review committee: A committee formed in a given hospital and comprised of physicians and other staff to review the quality of services rendered as well as the effective and appropriate use of facilities. See also *Professional Standards Review Organization*.

149

V

vaginismus: Involuntary spasms of the muscles surrounding the entrance to the vagina and part of the vagina itself occurring with real or imagined attempts at vaginal entry thereby obstructing penetration.

validity: See *Table of Research Terms*, p. 74.

variable (dependent and independent): See *Table of Research Terms*, p. 74.

vegetative nervous system: Obsolete term for the *autonomic nervous system*.

verbigeration: Stereotyped and seemingly meaningless repetition of words or sentences. See *perseveration*.

vertigo: A sensation of dizziness or "spinning around."

Vineland Social Maturity Scale: See *Table of Psychological Tests*, p. 78.

visceral learning: See *biofeedback*.

vitamin therapy: See *orthomolecular therapy*.

voluntary admission: See *commitment*.

voyeurism: Sexually motivated and often *compulsive* interest in watching or looking at others, particularly at genitals. A "peeping Tom" represents a pathological expression of voyeurism.

W

Watson, John B. (1878-1958): American *psychologist;* the founder of the *behaviorism* school of *psychology.*

waxy flexibility: See *cerea flexibilitas.*

Wechsler Adult Intelligence Scale (WAIS): See *Table of Psychological Tests,* p. 78.

Wechsler Intelligence Scale for Children (WISC): See *Table of Psychological Tests,* p. 78.

Wechsler Preschool and Primary Scale of Intelligence (WPPSI): See *Table of Psychological Tests,* p. 78.

weekend hospitalization. See *partial hospitalization.*

Wernicke-Korsakoff syndrome: A disorder of *central nervous system* metabolism due to a lack of vitamin B_1 (thiamin) seen in chronic *alcoholism.* Wernicke's disease features irregularities of eye movements, incoordination, impaired thinking, and often sensory-motor deficits. Korsakoff's *psychosis* is characterized by *confabulation* but, more importantly, grossly impaired memory function with deficient new learning ability. Wernicke's disease and Korsakoff's psychosis begin suddenly and are often found in the same person simultaneously.

Weyer, Johann (circa 1530): Dutch physician who was one of the first to devote his major interest to psychiatric disorders. Regarded by some as the founder of modern *psychiatry.*

White, William Alanson (1870-1937): American *psychiatrist* famous

151

for his early support of *psychoanalysis* and his contributions to *forensic psychiatry*.

windigo: See *culture specific syndromes*.

withdrawal: A pathological retreat from people or the world of reality, often seen in *schizophrenia*.

withdrawal symptoms: Physical and mental effects of withdrawing drugs from patients who have become habituated or addicted to them. The physical symptoms may include nausea, vomiting, tremors, abdominal pain, *delirium* and *convulsions*. See *addiction* and *delirium tremens*.

wordblindness: See *learning disability*.

word salad: A mixture of words and phrases that lack comprehensive meaning or logical coherence, commonly seen in *schizophrenic* states.

working through: Exploration of a problem by patient and therapist until a satisfactory solution has been found or until a symptom has been traced to its *unconscious* sources.

X

xenophobia: See *phobia*.

Z

zygosity (dizygotic and monozygotic): See *Table of Research Terms*, p. 74.

REFERENCES

Hinsie, Leland E., M.D., and Campbell, Robert J., M.D., *Psychiatric Dictionary*, Fourth Edition, Oxford University Press, New York, 1970.

Diagnostic and Statistical Manual of Mental Disorders, Second Edition (Seventh Printing, 1974), American Psychiatric Association, Washington, D.C., 1968.

Dorland's Illustrated Medical Dictionary, Twenty-Fifth Edition, W. B. Saunders, Co., Philadelphia, 1974.

A Glossary of Psychoanalytic Terms and Concepts, Edited by Burness E. Moore, M.D. and Bernard D. Fine, M.D., The American Psychoanalytic Association, New York, 1967.

The Committee on Public Information 1952-1974

Edward G. Billings, M.D.
Wilfred Bloomberg, M.D., *Chairman*, 1952-1954
*John P. Briggs, M.D.
James P. Cattell, M.D., *Chairman*, 1973-1974
Rives Chalmers, M.D.
Irvin M. Cohen, M.D.
Robert Coles, M.D.
*Nicholas P. Dallis, M.D.
Edward M. Daniels, M.D.
J. Lawrence Evens, M.D.
David J. Flicker, M.D.
*Shervert Frazier, M.D.
Irving Gail, M.D.
Edward O. Harper, M.D.
L. Lee Hasenbush, M.D.
Robert O. Jones, M.D.
Henry P. Laughlin, M.D., *Chairman*, 1957-1961
Zigmond M. Lebensohn, M.D., *Chairman*, 1964-1967, 1970-1973
*Myron H. Marshall, M.D.
D. G. McKerracher, M.D.
Robert T. Morse, M.D., *Chairman*, 1955-1958, 1961-1964.
   Deceased, February 18, 1964
J. Martin Myers, M.D., *Chairman*, 1967-1969
Henry P. Pechstein, M.D.
James K. Peden, M.D.
Seymour Perlin, M.D.
*Eric Plaut, M.D.
Myrick W. Pullen, M.D.
C. A. Roberts, M.D.
Benjamin Simon, M.D.
Rogers J. Smith, M.D.
Robert A. Solow, M.D.
Marvin Stern, M.D.
*John A. Talbott, M.D.
William G. Tompkins, M.D.
*Arnold Werner, M.D., *Chairman*, 1974-
Donovan G. Wright, M.D.
David A. Young, M.D.

Indicates present members (1974)

AMERICAN PSYCHIATRIC ASSOCIATION

FOUNDED IN 1844

The Oldest National Medical Society in the United States

The objects of this Association are:

—to improve the treatment, rehabilitation, and care of the mentally ill, the mentally retarded, and the emotionally disturbed;

—to promote research, professional education in psychiatry and allied fields, and the prevention of psychiatric disabilities;

—to advance the standards of all psychiatric services and facilities;

—to foster the cooperation of all who are concerned with the medical, psychological, social, and legal aspects of mental health and illness; and

—to make psychiatric knowledge available to other practitioners of medicine, to scientists in other fields of knowledge, and to the public.

157